Recipes from South Africa

Written by Lizel Salter
Pictures by Martin Salter, Lizel Salter,
My Mother Alet Willer, My Sister Corlia and
Auntie Sophia.

**The Book, Website, Photos and Content are all
protected under the
copyright © of Lizel Salter and IYC Limited.
All rights reserved - 2009.**

D1334627

TABLE OF CONTENTS

1. Introduction 6

2. Short History of South Africa 11

3. Thanks and Enjoy 14

4. Cooking Terms 15
    4.1 Weights and Measures 15
    4.2 Oven Temperature 15
    4.3 Substitutes 15

5. Starters 16
    5.1 Peri-Peri Chicken Livers 17
    5.2 Liver with Sour Sauce 18
    5.3 Tuna Salad with Lettuce 18
    5.4 Ham and Cheese Rolls 19
    5.5 Bacon Bites ("Spekkies") 19

6. BBQ Recipes ("Braaivleis") 20
    The "Braai" (BBQ) 21
    6.1 Crumbly Mealy Maze Porridge 22
        6.1.1 Crumbly Mealy Porridge 23
        6.1.2 "Stywe Pap" 23
    6.2 Boer's Sausages ("Boerewors") 24
    6.3 Skewers 25
        6.3.1 Skewers in Marinade ("Sosaties") 26
    6.4 Porridge (Maize Meal) Tart ("Paptert") 27
    6.5 Mealy Bake 28
    6.6 Grilled Bread ("Roosterkoek") 28
    6.7 Toasted Sandwiches ("Braaibroodjies") 29

7. Main Dishes 30
    7.1 Fish Dish ("Gesmoorde snoek") 31
    7.2 History of Bobotie 31
        7.2.1 Mince Bobotie 32
        7.2.2 Chicken Bobotie 33
    7.3 Chicken in Sauce 34
    7.4 Chicken Pie 35
    7.5 Ox Tongue 36
    7.6 Meatballs ("Frikkadelle") 37
    7.7 Durbs Meat Bunny Chow 38
    7.8 Vegetarian Bunny Chow 39
    7.9 Great Curry 40

7.10 History of "Potjiekos" 41
      7.10.1 "Potjiekos" 42
7.11 Water Lily Stew ("Waterblommetjiebredie") 43
7.12 Tomato Stew ("Tamatiebredie") 44
7.13 "Chakalaka" 45
7.14 Dried Meat 45
      7.14.1 Biltong 46
      7.14.2 Dried Sausages ("Droë Wors") 47

8. Side Dishes **48**
8.1 Yellow Rice 49
8.2 Biltong and Cheese Pot Bread 50
8.3 Potato Cakes 50
8.4 Cinnamon Dumplings ("Souskluitjies") 51
8.5 Potato Mealy Dish 52
8.6 Cream Spinach 52
8.7 Warm Potato Dish 53
8.8 Sweet Potato in Sauce 54
8.9 Pumpkin and Mushroom Dish 54
8.10 Salted Yellow Carrots 55
8.11 Pumpkin Fritters ("Pampoenkoekies") 56

9. Salads **57**
9.1 "Snoek" Salad (Fish) 58
9.2 Tuna Noodle Salad 58
9.3 Curry Noodle Salad 59
9.4 Chicken and Avocado Salad 59
9.5 Potato Salad 60
9.6 Beetroot Salad 60
9.7 Three Bean Salad 61
9.8 Pea Salad 62
9.9 Curry Carrot Salad 62
9.10 Carrot and Pineapple Salad 63
9.11 Fruit Boat Salad 64
9.12 Green Mixed Salad 64
9.13 Banana Salad 65

10. Sauces **66**
10.1 Monkey Gland Sauce 67
10.2 Sweet and Sour Sauce 67
10.3 Basic White Sauce 68
10.4 Cheese and Onion Sauce 68
10.5 Mushroom and Cheese Sauce 69
10.6 Peri-Peri Sauce 70
10.7 Bar One Sauce (Mars Bar) 70
10.8 Wine Sauce 71

11. Warm Desserts **72**
    11.1 Sago Pudding 73
    11.2 Bread Pudding 73
    11.3 Bread and Butter Pudding 74
    11.4 Cottage Pudding 75
    11.5 Roly-Poly 76
    11.6 Leap Year Pudding 76
    11.7 "Doek" Pudding 77
    11.8 "Malva" Pudding 78
    11.9 Floating Island Dessert 79

12. Cold Desserts **80**
    12.1 Dom Pedro 81
    12.2 Yoghurt Pudding 82
    12.3 Set Pear Pudding 82
    12.4 Cookie Ice Cream Pudding 82
    12.5 Home Made Cheesecake 83
    12.6 Trifle 84
    12.7 Chocolate Mousse 85
    12.8 Home Made Cape Velvet 86

13. Special Treats **87**
    13.1 "Vetkoek" 88
    13.2 Coconut Ice 89
    13.3 Pancakes 90
    13.4 Rainbow Sandwiches 90
    13.5 "Plaatkoekies" (like Crumpets) 91
    13.6 Cinnamon Toast 92
    13.7 Cheese Puffs 93
    13.8 Microwave Fudge 93
    13.9 Scones 94
    13.10 "Ystervarkies" 95
    13.11 Jam Tarts ("Handtertjies") 96
    13.12 Meringue ("Skuimpies") 97
    13.13 Chocolate Treat 97
    13.14 "Melkkos" 98
    13.15 "Koeksisters" 99

14. Cookies and Rusks **100**
    14.1 Boer's Rusks ("Boerbeskuit") 101
    14.2 Buttermilk Rusks 102
    14.3 Old Fashioned Sweet Cookies 103
    14.4 1-2-3 Easy to Make Sweet Cookies 103
    14.5 Coffee Cookies 104

14.6 Rice Crispy Cookies 105
14.7 Oats Cookies 105
14.8 Ginger Cookies 106
14.9 Peanut Butter Cookies 106
14.10 Apricot Cookies 107
14.11 Custard Cookies 108
14.12 Apricot Squares 109
14.13 Cherry and Rice Crispy Cookies 109
14.14 "Soentjies" (Kisses) 110
14.15 Jan Smuts Cookies 111
14.16 Home-Made Romany Creams 112
14.17 General Hertzog Cookies 113

15. Bread **114**
15.1 Date Bread 115
15.2 Raisin Bread 115
15.3 Banana Bread 116
15.4 Gingerbread 117
15.5 Mealy Bread 117

16. Preserves (Jams) and Chutney **118**
16.1 Apricot Preserve 119
16.2 Watermelon Preserve 120
16.3 Guava Preserve 121
16.4 Peach Chutney 121
16.5 Marmalade 121
16.6 Green Fig Preserve 122

17. Tarts **123**
17.1 Cramora Tart 124
17.2 Guava Fridge Tart 124
17.3 Milk Tart ("Melktert") 125
17.4 Pineapple Tart 126
17.5 Peppermint Crisp Tart 126
17.6 Apple Tart 127
17.7 Yoghurt Tart 127
17.8 Marshmallow Tart 128
17.9 Tipsy Tart 129
17.10 Savoury Tart 130

18. Cakes **131**
18.1 Chocolate Cake 132
18.2 Fruit Cake 133
18.3 Sponge Cake 134
18.4 Carrot Cake 135

1. INTRODUCTION

Another recipe book you might say, but this one is special. Let me tell you why . . .

I decided to write this book, not just to share with you the recipes I grew up with, and so my mother, grandmother and all of my family before me, but to give you an insight into South African lives. A history of where we come from, how we managed to become our own country, our own people, and our individual personality. What started off as a lot of people with different backgrounds put together in one place, ended up as one nation, united in pride and the amazing feeling of belonging, knowing that you are South African and understanding what that means.

Being South African means that, no matter where in the world you are, you will always be a South African, love your country with all that you are and remembering everything you grew up with, specially the food!! That, besides my mother, family and friends of course, must be what I miss most, living in another country. No one can cook like my mother!! But luckily all South African girls grow up learning how to cook and most importantly, how to **BAKE**!!

I will start this book by sharing with you the 9 provinces in our great country and giving you a brief background on the history of South Africa. The history of our traditional South African recipes can be found at the recipes itself.

If you ever feel homesick, just look at these beautiful pictures of our lovely country and remember where you come from . . .

Balito

The beautiful coastal city of Balito is located on the eastern side of the country very close to Durban. **KwaZulu Natal** is a beautiful province that experiences eternal summer. It has a tropical climate with a very generous rainfall during the summer months. During these months, it can get extremely hot and humid along the coastline. Average temperatures during the winter can be as high as 22°C. A fantastic holiday destination throughout the year.

Balito is also very well known for dolphins and if you watch closely during the very early morning or late afternoon hours, you might just be spoilt with seeing them swim past...

If you are driving from Gauteng to visit this beautiful KwaZulu Natal province, you will have to drive for around 6 hours, very exhausting, but at least you have to go over one of the greatest passes in South Africa. Van Reenen's Pass is breathtaking and something to experience. Have a look and see if you would want to miss this beautiful view?

Van Reenen

Limpopo province is named after the great Limpopo River. It is the most northern part of South Africa and borders onto Zimbabwe, Botswana and Mozambique. The northern section of Kruger National Park is located in Limpopo and you will also find the great Soutpansberg Mountain range.

Limpopo has very hot but yet pleasant summers and dry winters. The sun shines almost year-round with a summer rainfall. The average summer temperatures are around 27 - 30°C (it can be higher).

Clarence

Clarence is in the Golden Gate Nature reserve, located in the **Free State** very close to the Lesotho border. The Golden Gate refers to the very impressive sandstone cliffs found on either side of the valley at the Golden Gate Dam. Here you can also find many caves and shelters displaying San rock paintings.

Views of Free State

The Free State is a summer rainfall area and it is warm in the summer but very cold in the winter months. Temperatures drop to around 9°C or less. The areas to the west and south of this province are semi-desert. It is a wonderful place to visit and there is nothing as beautiful as a sunset in the Free State…

Sundown in Free State

Gauteng is the smallest province that offers one of the world's best climates. During the summer months, days are very warm, but mostly wind-free. In the winter, the days are crisp and clear. It has a summer-rainfall with hot summers and winters with frost. Hail is very common during the summer thunderstorms. Gauteng is also known for its "electric storms" where the lightning lights up the skies and the thunder is overwhelming, but no rain falls, leaving an amazing smell in the air. Snowfall rarely occurs during the winter, but is possible.

One of the biggest and most important Dams in the country is located in Gauteng and is known as the Vaal Dam. It lies on the Vaal River, which is one of South Africa's strongest-flowing rivers. Water from this dam is used to supply drinking water to Gauteng and environs. The dam has a surface area of 300 square kilometres and is about 47 metres deep!

Vaal Dam

Simply South African

This is a very important and valuable dam. During the dry seasons the dam is very empty. When this picture was taken, 8 sluices had to be opened. During the period up until 2 weeks before this picture was taken, the dam was only 6% full. Unbelievable!

The southern part of the Kruger National Park can be found in **Mpumalanga**. This province has hot summers with a summer rainfall and mild winters. It can become very cold in the Highveld areas.

Sun City as well as Pilanesberg National Park is located in the **North West** province. A great holiday destination whether you want to visit for only one day or maybe a few weeks. Here you can enjoy hot summers with sunny days. Average temperatures vary between 25 - 34°C. The winter days can be relatively warm, but during the evenings and early morning, it can be chilly. Rainfall is during the summer.

This brings us to the fairest Cape, also known as the Cape of storms…

Table Mountain is very easily identified. This is the "table" of the Cape, very flat and sometimes covered with a little "tablecloth", or better known as mist! How can you ever visit South Africa without going up in a cable car and experiencing the magnificent view from the tabletop?

The Cape is divided into three separate provinces. The first is the **Western Cape**, where Table Mountain and Robin Island is situated. At the most Southern point of South Africa you will see where the two oceans (Atlantic and Indian) meet. This is one of the reasons why the Cape is known as the Cape of Storms. Many ships have been destroyed in this area…

The Western Cape enjoys hot summers and mild, green winters due to the winter rainfall. The weather here is ideal for the production of fruit, wine and grains. Average temperatures are around 26°C, but it can get cold in the winter, especially in the mornings!

The **Northern Cape** is a semi-arid region with only a little rainfall during the spring/summer months. For two months of the year during August and September this desert area is transformed into a flower paradise. Namakwaland is something great and should be experienced. During the winter months it is extremely cold and frosty, while VERY high temperatures are experienced during the summer months. Temperatures range between -6°C in the winter and anything from 30°C upward in the summer.

The **Eastern Cape** enjoys hot summers and moderate winters with a summer rainfall. Maximum summer temperatures on average are around 27°C while the minimum temperature in winter can be as low as 7°C or less.

Now you know a little bit about each of the 9 provinces. If you want to know more, you will have to visit and try the great food and wine while you are there!

You can also visit my **blog** at www.RecipesFromSouthAfrica.com/blog for more information about places to visit in South Africa.

2. SHORT HISTORY OF SOUTH AFRICA

The first inhabitants date back around 10 000 years. The San (also known as the Bushmen) were skilled hunter-gatherers, gathering food according to what was available. Later on, their hunting gave way to herding as their dominant economic activity, including small herds of cattle and oxen. The San made the most beautiful rock paintings using natural pigments. They were nomadic, never settling down, always on the move. Even today they still move around, but they are more settled and their lifestyles are very different.

Around 6 000 years later 2 groups, the Hottentot and Khoikhoi, moved down from the northern parts of Africa with their cattle and sheep, and didn't have any conflict with the San people. They settled around the Cape Province. By the 17th century the Bantu and Xhosas moved into the Eastern Cape area, moving down from central Africa. This is the time that the Europeans arrived.

The first to arrive in South Africa were the Portuguese explorers, lead by Bartolomeu Dias, wishing to find a sea route to India and Asia. They rounded the Cape in 1487 and anchored in Mossel Bay. Vasco Da Gama arrived at St. Helena Bay in 1498. In 1510 he lost a lot of men to the Hottentots and moved on to Mozambique.

But it was the Dutch that would come to dominate the sea lines. In 1647 a Dutch vessel was destroyed by the great waves and the crew set up camp on the shores for one year, awaiting rescue. They decided to establish a secure camp where passing ships could shelter, sailors could rest and stock up on fresh supplies of food for their further journey.

Jan van Riebeeck lead this group and arrived on 6th April 1652 in Table Bay. They set themselves up as self-sufficient farmers, growing wheat, vegetables and vines. More people came, mostly Dutch, but also some Belgians, Scandinavians and Germans. Around 1688 the French also arrived, Protestants that were fleeing religious persecution back in their home country.

These early settlers were short of labour, and slaves were imported from Guinea, Angola, Delgoa Bay, Java, Madagascar and Malaysia. There was now a big mixture of races and languages. They were absorbed and a new community was created, all learning to speak the new language. A mixture of Dutch and Afrikaans was born. The Cape coloureds were born when the slaves from Indonesia and Madagascar married the Dutch.

The "Trekboere" (farmers that moved around) from European descent moved away from Cape Town, more inland. They were semi-nomadic and moved around, only having a wagon, tent, a Bible and some guns. They lived independently and totally free from official controls.

The British troops arrived in 1795 and they took over control of the Cape in 1814. They brought over thousands of English people to settle there and a second language and culture were introduced to the country. The uneducated "Boere" were not happy, being told what to do by people from another country and decided to move even further inland to get away from their rule.

Wanting to establish their own independent state, they started the Great "Trek". The "Voortrekkers" at this stage, split into 2 groups. One moved northwards and the other to eastern Natal, but this land was already taken by the Zulu's.

Their king, Shaka, had bonded his people very closely and had a strong nation of warriors. Around them were also living Venda, Tsonga, Sotho, Pedi and Tswana people. Piet Retief, the leader of the "Voortrekkers" went to negotiate some land from Dingaan. After an agreement was reached, Dingaan killed Piet Retief and his party. On 16 December 1838 the "Boere" and the Zulu's fought the battle of Blood River, leaving many "Boere" injured and thousands of Zulu's dead.

In 1843 the British took over control of Natal as well and the "Boere" moved to Transvaal and the Orange Free State. The first "Boer" War against the British followed in 1880 which the "Boere" won. Transvaal and Orange Free State became independent "Boer" states.

When gold was discovered in Johannesburg, the British wanted to have a part of this great wealth so the second "Boer" War followed in 1899. More than 450 000 British troops fought against 50 000 "Boer" rebellions (as they were called) for 2 and a half years. By the end of the war around 20 000 British troops and 6 000 "Boer" fighters were killed. In consentration camps more than 20 000 Black people fighting with the "Boere", 5 000 white woman and 22 000 children under the age of 16 lost their lives. In 1902 the war was ended with the "Boere" putting down their weapons, not wanting to see anymore of their family killed in these camps.

In 1925 the British agreed to have Afrikaans as a second official language together with English. South Africa became a Republic on the 31st of May 1961 and apartheid was introduced. During the years that followed, Black people in South Africa had a very difficult time and were treated unfairly by White rule. But in 1994, South Africa had it's first democratic election, Mister Nelson Mandela became President and apartheid became something of the past.

Looking at this colourful history, one thing is very clear. We as a country have been through so much together, it just makes us a stronger unit, a very proud nation! We have many different cultures and nationalities that settled in South Africa and still, everyone living there is uniquely South African with their own languages and culture, nothing like the countries they came from.

All of them brought something with them: their knowledge. The Malaysian slaves brought their spices, the Dutch their methods of cooking, the Portuguese their Peri-Peri and the British their roast potatoes. Without any of these nationalities of people coming to South Africa, our recipes would not be possible. Although they are all proudly South African, the ingredients are mixed, brought over by different people.

Most of the recipes in this book are "Boerekos" (Boer food, made by Voortrekkers) becauce that is my heritage, but there are also other favourite South African recipes.

3. THANKS AND ENJOY!

I hope this book (1st printed edition) will mean as much to people from other countries, as it will to my fellow countrymen and women. Good food can be enjoyed by everyone, it doesn't matter where you live. Take these easy to cook recipes and enjoy. South Africans who love cooking and baking will find any occasion a reason to do so. "Braai" rules everytime! (Barbecue to the English readers out there).

I would also like to take one moment to thank every single person that helped me to gather all these recipes. Most of them are thanks to my lovely mother, who introduced me to them. Thank you also to friends and family who contributed, specially my Aunt. Without all of you this would have been impossible. My husband, mother, sister and Aunt Sophia helped me with the great pictures you will see throughout.

A great special thank you goes out to my wonderful husband Martin who helped me to get started in writing my book and putting everything together. He is the one who convinced me to not only sell a downloadable version of my book, but also a real one.

My last but not least thank you goes out to our beautiful little baby boy Marius. He arrived 3 ½ weeks early just one week ago and weighed only 2.55 kg, but he is our bundle of love and joy and having our own little family inspires me to cook even more and better.

This book is for all of you!! Enjoy every moment and I hope that this recipe book will mean as much to you as it does to me.

Lizel Salter

14

4. COOKING TERMS

4.1 WEIGHTS AND MEASURES

I tried to keep the measurements as easy as possible. For the sake of uniformity, I chose to make use of cups, tablespoons and teaspoons. Dry ingredients have already been converted to cups.

The following can be used as a guide:

1 cup	a cup that holds 250ml of liquid
¾ cup	188ml
½ cup	125ml
¼ cup	63ml
Pinch	¼ of a teaspoon (usually salt or pepper)
1 teaspoon	holds 5ml of fluid
1 tablespoon	holds 12.5ml of fluid

Butter will be measured in cups:

2 cups	500g (1 pound)
1 cup	250g (½ pound)
½ cup	125g (¼ pound)
¼ cup	62.5g (1/8 pound)

4.2 OVEN TEMPERATURES

In South Africa we all use electric ovens, so the °C should not be a problem. Our friends and fellow countrymen living in other countries might have trouble. Therefore I decided to write down the temperature in both °C and gas mark. In England I know, gas ovens are being used everyday.

120°C	Gas mark 1
150°C	Gas mark 2
160°C	Gas mark 3
180°C	Gas mark 4
190°C	Gas mark 5
200°C – 220°C	Gas mark 6
230°C – 260°C	Gas mark 7 – 8

4.3 SUBSTITUTES

When you bake, you can substitute the cake flour and baking powder for self-raising flour. One thing I discover in England is that the flour is much heavier than in South Africa. I would recommend that you use self-raising flour as well as baking powder instead of regular cake flour.

5. Starters

Peri-Peri Chicken Livers

Liver with
Sour Sauce

Tuna Salad
with Lettuce

Ham and Cheese Rolls

Bacon Bites ("Spekkies")

5.1 PERI-PERI CHICKEN LIVERS

Peri-Peri is most definitely a great gift from the Portuguese. Their love for Peri-Peri meant that South Africans adopted this uniquely strong taste and made it their own by adding it to chicken livers, prawns and chicken wings - a taste so great that it is even added to steaks in restaurants today! Watch out though, this sauce is VERY HOT!!

Ingredients
2 tablespoons vegetable oil
1 large chopped onion
2 crushed garlic cloves
2 fresh chillies, de-seeded and chopped (green or red, depending whether you
        like it hot or mild)
½ teaspoon Peri-Peri powder or cayenne pepper
1 teaspoon ginger
500g chicken livers
1 chopped tomato
Salt and pepper to taste
½ cup dry white wine

Method
1. Heat the oil in a saucepan and add the onion, garlic and chillies. Sauté until soft and golden brown.
2. Add the Peri-Peri (or cayenne pepper) and ginger. Mix well.
3. Add the chicken livers and tomatoes and stir-fry over a high heat until the livers are just cooked.
4. Season with salt and pepper.
5. Add the wine and cook over a medium heat for 5 minutes.

To serve
Spoon the chicken livers into a little bowl. On the side, serve with a green salad and freshly baked, warm bread and butter. All you have to do now, is eat and enjoy.

You can also substitute the Peri-Peri powder with 1 teaspoon of turmeric and 1 tablespoon of curry if the Peri-Peri is too hot for your taste.

5.2 LIVER WITH SOUR SAUCE

Ingredients
500g livers
Salt and pepper
1 tablespoon oil
1 cup boiling water
Mushrooms
1 tablespoon flour
1 tablespoon sugar
1 ½ tablespoons vinegar

Method
1. Clean the livers and cut into pieces.
2. Sprinkle the livers with salt and pepper and fry in a little bit of oil for about 5 minutes.
3. Add the boiling water and mushrooms.
4. Simmer for about 10 minutes.
5. Mix the flour, sugar and vinegar together, and add to the liver.
6. Let it boil for about 5 minutes and keep stirring until the sauce is thick.

5.3 TUNA SALAD WITH LETTUCE

Ingredients
400g of tuna in a tin
2 tablespoons mayonnaise
½ onion, diced
½ green pepper, diced
Lettuce
Parsley

Method
1. Mix the tuna with mayonnaise.
2. Add the diced onion and green pepper.
3. Mix very well.

To serve
1. Place big pieces of lettuce in a little bowl.
2. Scoop spoons full of the tuna mixture onto the lettuce.
3. Garnish with parsley.

18

5.4 HAM AND CHEESE ROLLS

Ingredients
2 teaspoons of pepper carrots (for each slice)
2 teaspoons grated cheese (for each slice)
Little bit of cream
6 thick slices of ham (enough for 2 people)
Lettuce
Mayonnaise
3 hard-boiled eggs (enough for all 6)

Method
1. Mix the carrots and grated cheese with enough cream, making sure the mixture is not too runny.
2. Place this mixture on the ham and roll up. Use a toothpick to keep the ham in place.
3. Place the ham on a bed of lettuce.
4. Smear the mayonnaise on top of the ham.
5. Sprinkle the yolk of the hard-boiled eggs on top of the mayonnaise.

5.5 BACON BITES ("SPEKKIES")

Ingredients
500g bacon
1 chopped onion
2 cups flour
2 teaspoons baking powder
Salt and cayenne pepper
1 teaspoon mustard powder
2 teaspoons parsley
2 cups grated cheddar cheese
1 beaten egg
1 ½ cups of milk

Method
1. Fry the bacon and place it on brown paper to drain the oil.
2. Fry the onion in the same pan that you fried the bacon in.
3. Sieve the dry ingredients together and add the bacon and onion.
4. Add the parsley and cheese.
5. Mix the egg and milk. Add to mixture.
6. Deep fry spoons full in warm oil until brown.

6. BBQ Recipes

THE "BRAAI" (BBQ)

With our lovely warm summers and dry, cold winters, South Africa can be labelled an "outdoors" country. Therefore we will have a "*braai*" in the winter and summer, come rain or shine! This must be the best excuse for socialising with your friends and family for a whole afternoon.

A "*braai*" is a very lengthy social affair. Men have time to discuss the rugby that will be played at about 17:00 that afternoon, a can of Castle (beer) in the hand, while spending the whole day outside, soaking up the sunshine. The woman have the opportunity to catch up with the latest from friends and family while preparing a lovely potato salad, "*braaibroodjies*" (bread toasted over the open flames) and maybe a mixed salad.

Many South Africans, black and white, would happily go through their whole lives living on meat and maize alone. They go together, hand in hand. A perfect "*braai*" would have to be "*boerewors*" with a lamb chop, "*sosaties*", "*braaibroodjies*", *pap* (made with maize meal) and sauce, foil-wrapped potatoes amongst the coals, potato salad and a mixed green salad. You can even grill bread on the fire while the meat is grilling! HEAVEN to any South African.

If you do not have a BBQ (braai) you can just put a few bricks together. It is very easy and there is never an excuse not to have one…

6.1 KRUMMEL PAP EN SOUS (Crumbly maize porridge and sauce)

Writing about this side "dish" is difficult. It is not easy to explain what *"mieliepap"* is. It is directly translated as maize porridge, but it is not what the Europeans or Americans know as porridge. It can be better described as polenta.

Maize is Africa's traditional and most important staple food, just like rice and noodles are for the East. It is also used as feed for livestock and is a great source of carbohydrates for both humans and animals. Most of South African landmass is planted with maize. Around 8 million metric tons of mealies are produced yearly (depending on the rainfall), 7.5 million are consumed while the surplus is exported to countries like Lesotho and Swaziland.

Mealies are planted in South Africa during November and harvested around March. Because mealies are very sensitive to drought, you never know how the crops will do until after the summer rains. The possible shortages in mealies can cause prices to rise sharply the following year.

Mealies were grown by Tribes long before Jan van Riebeeck ever came to South Africa. This wonderful mealies as well as the flour used in porridge was taken to the *"Voortrekkers"* hearts when they were moving inland and has been a favourite ever since.

This maize porridge can be served in many forms by adding varying amounts of water and salt. Depending on what the water and maize meal ratio is, the *"pap"* can be served for breakfast (ratio of 1 cup of meal to 3 cups of water) with butter, sugar and milk. It can also be served as a side dish with a *"braai"* where the ratio of maize meal is higher as previously mentioned. *"Pap"* at a *"braai"* is served with a savoury sauce!

I will give you both recipes for *"krummelpap"* as well as *"stywepap"*. Not everybody likes *"krummelpap"*. The big difference lies in the ratio again as well as stirring the *"pap"*.

6.1.1 CRUMBLY MAIZE MEAL ("Krummelpap")

Ingredients

2 cups water
½ teaspoon salt

3 cups of maize meal
1 teaspoon butter

Method
1. Bring the water and salt to the boil.
2. Add the maize meal to the boiling water *WITHOUT* stirring.
3. Place the lid on top and let it simmer for about 20 minutes over a low heat.
4. Stir with a fork until meal is crumbly.
5. Put the lid back on and let it simmer for another 20 minutes. Stir again.
6. Make sure the *"pap"* simmers for another 20 minutes over a very low heat.
7. Add the butter before serving.

6.1.2 RIGID, NOT CRUMBLY ("Stywepap")

Ingredients

4 cups water
Pinch of salt

2 cups of maize meal
1 teaspoon butter

Method
1. Bring the water and salt to the boil.
2. Add the maize meal and stir thoroughly with a wooden spoon. Close the lid.
3. Turn the heat right down and let it simmer for 30 minutes, stirring occasionally.
4. Add ½ a cup of cold water and simmer for another 30 minutes.
5. Add the butter, stir and serve.

Ingredients for the sauce

2 tablespoons of butter
1 onion (cut in rings)
3 tomatoes - skin removed and chopped
(you can also use tinned tomatoes)
½ cup peach chutney
1 tablespoon Worcestershire sauce

¼ cup tomato sauce
¼ cup white vinegar
1 tablespoon mustard
2 tablespoons brown sugar
½ teaspoon salt

Method
1. Fry the onion in the butter until light brown.
2. Add the tomatoes and let it simmer for about 5 minutes.
3. Mix the rest of the ingredients and add to the onion and tomato mix.
4. Let it simmer for another 5 minutes over a low heat. Pour warm over *pap*!

6.2 BOER'S SAUSAGE ("Boerewors")

Boeries (as boerewors is known by South Africans) is a part of our culture. It is a legacy from early German settlers, passed on through their love for spicy *wurst*. The basic idea of sausages was taken from the Germans and by adding our own spices, beef and fat, "*boerewors*" was "invented". No self-respecting "*braai*" can ever be without it! The secret to making "*boerewors*", lies in the quality of the ingredients that you use. The better the quality, the better the "*boerewors*" will taste.

Ingredients

2kg beef
1kg pork
500g pork fat
2 tablespoons salt
1 teaspoon pepper
1 teaspoon cayenne pepper
4 tablespoons of ground coriander

½ teaspoon grated walnut
½ teaspoon ground cloves
½ teaspoon ground dried thyme
½ teaspoon ground allspice
½ cup of vinegar
85g sausage casings

Method
1. Grind the meat by using a medium-course grinding plate.
2. Cut the pork fat into little cubes and add to the meat.
3. Mix all the spices, salt and pepper and sprinkle over the meat.
4. Add vinegar and let it stand for 1 hour.
5. Let the sausage casings soak in water while you wait for this hour to pass.
6. Mix it again and fill the sausage casings firmly. Make sure it is not filled too tightly with the mixture.
7. "*Braai*" outside on the fire (BBQ) or in the oven.
8. Makes about 3.5kg.

6.3 SKEWERS OR KEBABS ("Sosaties")

The word "*sosatie*" comes from a combination of *sate* (skewered meat) and *saus* (spicy sauce). It is from Cape Malay origin, used in Afrikaans, which is the primary language of the Cape Malays.

Mutton chunks are marinated in a lovely sauce over night (or longer) and then put on the "*braai*". The result is gloriously tasty meat with a marinade that is wonderfully tacky! Be warned: you will be sticky from ear to ear, but smiling at the same time! You can use any meat of your choice.

It is important that when you make these sosaties you let the meat marinade over night. It will give more taste and flavour to the meat and the meat will be very soft and lovely to eat.

Before you make the "*sosaties*", make sure to soak the wooden skewers in water for a few hours. This will stop the skewers from burning when you place them on the BBQ.

Making "*sosaties*" do take some time, but I can promise you that it is definitely worth the trouble. It is the best kebab you will **EVER** taste…

6.3.1 SKEWERS IN MARINADE (Serves about 12 people)

1kg lamb
1kg pork (you can also use chicken)
2 onions, quartered

1 of each green, red and yellow pepper
Mushrooms (3 for each skewer)

You will also need skewers to put the meat on.

Marinade

2 onions
1 tablespoon curry
1 tablespoon turmeric
2 tablespoons brown sugar
Salt and pepper
1 cup white vinegar
¾ cup of water

1 teaspoon ginger
1 teaspoon cinnamon
1 teaspoon coriander
½ teaspoon freshly ground cloves
1 tablespoon of cornflour
½ cup dried apricots (or apricot chutney)
2 lemon leaves

Method

1. Make up your skewers by cutting the meat into cubes. Place the meat, peppers, mushrooms and onions on a skewer (6 cubes of meat per skewer).
2. *Marinade:* Cut the 2 onions into rings and boil them in a little water. After you have drained the water, add butter and fry it until light brown.
3. Mix the curry, turmeric, sugar, salt, vinegar, the rest of the spices and cornflour together and add to the onions.
4. Add the apricots (or chutney) and boil together for 3 minutes. Remove and let it cool down.
5. Add the lemon leaves and place the skewers in the sauce. Leave for about 2 days in the refrigerator. Make sure you turn the skewers each day (skewers can be left in the refrigerator over night. The longer you leave it, the softer the meat will be).
6. Grill the skewers over the "*braai*". Heat up the sauce and serve with the "*sosaties*".

6.4 PORRIDGE (MAIZE MEAL) TART ("Paptert")

Ingredients for "pap"
3 cups water
1 cup maize meal
Pinch of salt

Method
1. Bring the water to the boil.
2. Add the salt to the maize meal and mix with a bit of water so the mixture is smooth when it is added to the boiling water.
3. Add to the boiling water and stir very well.
4. Turn the heat right down and place the lid on top.
5. Let the maize meal cook for about 5 minutes, stirring every now and again.

Ingredients for maize tart
Prepared "pap" (maize meal) from top
1 pack of bacon (finely cut)
1 green pepper (chopped)
10 mushrooms (chopped)
1 tinned tomato and onion
1 tin sweet corn
Grated cheese

Method
1. Fry the bacon, green pepper and mushrooms together.
2. Add the tinned tomato and onion and the sweet corn and let it cook for about 3 minutes while stirring.
3. Use a square glass bowl. First add halve the "*pap*" and then halve the filling mixture. Repeat and then sprinkle grated cheese on top.
4. Bake in a pre-heated oven at 170°C for about 20 minutes or until the cheese is melted.

6.5 MEALY BAKE

Ingredients
4 eggs
2 tablespoons sugar
¼ cup melted butter
¼ cup flour
3 teaspoons baking powder
2 tins of creamy sweet corn

Method
1. Beat the eggs and sugar together.
2. Add the melted butter and mix.
3. Mix the rest of the ingredients in with the mixture.
4. Bake in a pre-heated oven at 180ºC for 1 hour.

6.6 GRILLED BREAD ("Roosterkoek")

Ingredients
4 cups flour
4 teaspoons baking powder
1 teaspoon salt
1 tablespoon syrup
¼ cup oil
Luke-warm water

Method
1. Sieve the flour, baking powder and salt together.
2. Mix the syrup with a little bit of water and add.
3. Add the oil and mix.
4. Add the water to the mixture (start with ½ cup. If you need more, add another ½). Make sure the mixture is not runny.
5. Knead the dough and let it stand for 2 hours to rise.
6. Make 1 large bread or cut the dough into smaller pieces.
7. Put on the BBQ and grill until light brown on both sides or bake in the oven.

6.7 TOASTED BREAD ("Braaibroodjies") – SERVES 2

You might think that this is just a regular toasted sandwich, but believe me, it is not! The grilled sandwiches takes on the smell and taste of the smoke coming from the charcoal. There is just no comparison. Try and enjoy, it tastes great!

Ingredients
4 slices of bread (white or brown, as you prefer)
Butter
8 slices of tomato
Salt and pepper
Aromat
Onions, cut in rings
Grated cheddar cheese

Method
1. Butter all four slices of bread.
2. First add the tomato to 2 slices of the bread and sprinkle the salt, pepper and aromat to taste.
3. Place onions on top of the tomato.
4. Sprinkle grated cheese on top.
5. Place the other slice of bread on top of the cheese and grill outside over the BBQ.
6. Make sure the cheese is melted. Enjoy!

7. Main Dishes

Simply South African

7.1 GESMOORDE SNOEK

South Africans enjoy their fish and other seafood like prawns, sardines and oysters. It is a bit harder these days to enjoy fish as freely as you would like, with the waters off the Cape and Namibia under siege from foreign fishing trawlers. Over-fishing in their own waters has forced them to come to South Africa.

We are very fond of a funny looking fish, called Kingklip. It can be baked, fried or grilled. Snoek, a game fish, is another favourite and is usually smoked or put on the "*braai*", outside on the fire. Snoek goes with anything, but is usually served with rice, potatoes and vegetables like spinach and pumpkin.

Ingredients

500g dry Snoek	Worcestershire sauce
3 boiled potatoes	Ground black pepper and nutmeg
2 onions	

Method
1. Put the fish in a bowl of cold water over night with the meat side facing the bottom.
2. Pour the water off the next morning. Put in fresh water and add the potatoes. Let the fish boil until it is cooked.
3. Fry the onions in half the butter until they are light brown.
4. Mash the fish using a fork and remove any bones.
5. Cut the potatoes into little blocks.
6. Add both the potatoes and onions to the fish and mix well. Make sure it is warm.
7. Now add the Worcestershire sauce to taste, pepper, nutmeg and the remaining butter.

To serve
Serve the fish on a bed of boiled yellow rice. Spinach and pumpkin can be served as side dishes, or maybe a green salad?

7.2 BOBOTIE

The greatest contribution to South African cooking came from the Malay slaves, bringing with them their knowledge and a combination of sweet and sour as well as spicy sauces, curries, chutneys and blatjangs. The Malay curries are not as hot as Indian curries. These spices and tastes have become part of our food culture. Combining these spices with other great ingredients introduced another winning recipe.

7.2.1 MINCE BOBOTIE

Ingredients
2 large onions
1 tablespoon of sunflower oil
1 thick slice of brown bread
1 cup milk
2 ½ tablespoons strong curry powder
1 teaspoon turmeric
1 teaspoon ginger
1 tablespoon brown sugar
2 tablespoons apricot jam
2 almonds, quartered
¼ cup lemon juice (or vinegar)
2 teaspoons salt
½ teaspoon white pepper
¼ cup seedless raisins
1 green apple, grated
10 dried apricots, soaked and cut up (or a tin of apricots)
1kg mutton (minced beef can be used as substitute)
4 lemon leaves or dried bay leaves
2 eggs

Method
1. Pre-heat the oven to 180°C. Lightly fry the onions in the oil.
2. Soak the bread in half the milk and mash with a fork. Add to the onion.
3. Add the curry, turmeric, ginger, sugar, jam, almonds, lemon juice, salt, pepper and raisins.
4. Add the apple, apricots, mince and 1 cup of water. Let simmer for 15 minutes.
5. Place in an ovenproof dish. Push the lemon/bay leaves in on the top.
6. Beat the eggs and milk together and pour over the meat. Slightly lift it to allow the egg to run into the bobotie. Bake until brown on top (about 20 – 30 minutes).

7.2.2 CHICKEN BOBOTIE

Ingredients

A: 6 chicken breasts   2 whole cloves
       2 cups of water   Pinch of salt

B: 2 tablespoons of sunflower oil
       2 onions, finely chopped
       2 teaspoons ginger
       2 tablespoons brown sugar
       1 teaspoon curry
       1 teaspoon turmeric
       1 teaspoon salt
       Pinch of black pepper

C: 1 slice of brown bread soaked in ½ cup of chicken stock (from group A)
       6 chicken breasts from group A
       ½ cup apricots, drain of the syrup
       ¼ cup raisins
       2 tablespoons fruit chutney
       1 tablespoon apricot jam
       2 tablespoons tomato paste
       1 tablespoon white vinegar
       3 teaspoons Worcestershire sauce

D: 1 egg
       ½ cup fat free milk
       3 lemon leaves

Method

1. Boil all the ingredients in A together until the chicken is soft. Remove meat from bones and cut finely. Keep the chicken stock.
2. Heat up the oil in a pan and add the onions.
3. Add all the dry ingredients from B.
4. Mix all the ingredients from C together with the onion mix.
5. Boil together for 20 minutes on a low heat, stirring every now and again.
6. Remove from heat and place this in the saucepan over the chicken.
7. Beat the egg and milk from D together and pour over the meat.
8. Place the lemon leaves on top of the meat
9. Bake in a pre-heated oven at 180°C for 45 minutes.

To serve

Both Boboties are served with yellow rice and raisins. Side dishes that complement this dish are sweet potato, potato salad, mixed Greek Salad or cheesy garlic bread.

7.3 CHICKEN IN SAUCE

Ingredients
1 chicken
Salt and black pepper
Chicken spices

Sauce
1 cup pickles
2 tablespoons tomato sauce
2 cups red wine
½ cup brown sugar
2 tablespoons Worcestershire sauce
½ cup apricot jam or apricot/peach chutney

Method
1. Cut the chicken into pieces, season with salt, pepper and chicken spices. Place in water and chicken stock for about 20 minutes. Make sure you turn the chicken once.
2. Remove the chicken from the water and place in a pan.
3. Cut the pickles in little pieces and mix the rest of the ingredients for the sauce.
4. Pour the sauce over the chicken in the pan. Place the lid on the pan and bake in a pre-heated oven of 180°C for 1 hour.
5. Do not open the lid during this process.
6. Serve with rice and mixed salad or vegetables.

7.4 CHICKEN PIE

1. Steam a whole chicken, remove the skin and break the chicken from the bones.
2. Fry 1 pack of bacon, one finely chopped green pepper, 1 onion finely chopped, salt and pepper.
3. Add this mixture together with 1 packet of chicken casserole to the fine chicken and mix very well. Place mixture inside the pastry.

Ingredients for pastry
4 cups flour
2 cups **frozen** margarine/butter
Pinch of salt
2 teaspoons cream of tartar
Soda/ice cold water (about 2 cups)

Method
1. Grate the margarine in with the flour and salt and fold in with a knife.
2. Mix the cream of tartar with a little bit of water and add to the mixture.
3. Add just enough soda water, making sure it isn't runny. Add ½ cup at a time.
4. Cover the dough with a wet cold cloth and place in the refrigerator for 30 minutes.
5. Break off a piece of the dough and roll it out. Keep the rest of the dough in the refrigerator, not letting it get warm. Place the rolled out dough in a pan (can be any form).
6. Fill up with the chicken mix, and make a lid with the rest of the dough.
7. Use a fork to make a few holes in the lid and use a brush to smear milk on top.
8. Place in a pre-heated oven at about 180°C and bake until golden brown (about 20 – 30 minutes).
9. Serve the pie with rice, potato salad, mixed salad and maybe *"pampoenkoekies"*.

7.5 OX TONGUE WITH SAUCE

Ingredients
1 ½ kg ox tongue
2 cups boiling water
1 teaspoon salt
1 teaspoon pepper
1 tablespoon brown sugar
1 tablespoon grated onion
5 fresh cloves

Method
1. Add the tongue to the boiling water, salt, pepper, sugar, onion and cloves.
2. Cook for 50 minutes in a pressure cooker.
3. Remove the skin from the tongue.

Sauce
2 tablespoons flour
3 teaspoons mustard powder
2 tablespoons oil
½ cup sugar
Pinch of salt
1 cup water
1 cup mayonnaise
1 tablespoon lemon juice
¼ cup vinegar
Breadcrumbs

1. Mix the flour, mustard, oil, sugar, salt and water until the mixture is smooth, and bring to the boil.
2. Remove from heat and mix the mayonnaise, lemon juice and vinegar with this mixture.
3. Cut the tongue in thin strips. Place half the sauce over a layer of meat. Then place another layer of meat and add the rest of the sauce.
4. Sprinkle a handful of breadcrumbs over the top and place in a pre-heated oven of 190°C, for half an hour.

7.6 MEATBALLS ("Frikkadelle")

Ingredients

1kg of minced meat (beef)
1 thick slice of brown bread
¼ cup milk
¼ cup oats
1 onion, finely chopped
2 teaspoons salt
Pinch of pepper
½ teaspoon coriander
1 tablespoon lemon juice
1 tablespoon apricot jam
1 tablespoon sugar
1 egg

Method

1. Pre-heat the oven to 180°C.
2. Soak the bread in the milk. Mash the bread with a fork and add this as well as the oats, to the meat.
3. Add the onion and mix.
4. Add salt, pepper, coriander, lemon juice, apricot jam, sugar and beaten egg.
5. Mix everything very well together.
6. Roll little meatballs by using your hands.
7. Place on a tray and add a ¼ cup of boiling water.
8. Let it bake for about an hour, turning them over after 30 minutes.
9. Serve with *"pampoenkoekies"* (pumpkin fritters) and maybe some potatoes.

7.7 DURBS MEAT BUNNY CHOW (ORIGINATED FROM DURBAN AROUND THE EARLY 1900's)

Slaves from Indonesia, Malaysia and workers from India arrived in South Africa and they brought along their curry foods. This became a very big part of our cuisine. Indian restaurants were opened in the early 1900's. A curry served with bread was an inexpensive meal and became a favourite. *Bunny chow* used to be served as a vegetarian meal, but with time, people wanted to have meat curries, and therefore you can make *Bunny chow* with any filling you like.

Because of *apartheid*, Black people were not allowed to be seated in restaurants. Take-away's were allowed to be sold, but no disposable bowls were available. An entrepreneur, Mr Bunia from Durban came up with the idea of hollowing out half a loaf of bread, in order to have "packaging" for the curry. This take-away became known as the *Bunny chow*, named after himself. A brilliant plan and a form of take-away that has stayed with us over the years! This must be the most popular curry dish in South Africa!

Ingredients

1 white bread (the whole bread, NOT sliced)
500g mutton (or lamb)
Oil
2 onions
2 cloves of garlic
1 teaspoon ginger
1 teaspoon turmeric

1 tablespoon brown sugar
1 teaspoon curry powder
2 red chillies, finely chopped
1 teaspoon cumin seeds
1 tablespoon coriander
1 tin (410ml) coconut milk
Salt and pepper

Method

1. Slice the lamb into cubes and fry in a little oil until evenly coloured.
2. Remove the meat and set aside.
3. Cut one of the onions and mix with the garlic and ginger. Cut the other onion in rings and fry in the oil used for the meat. Add the first onion mix and fry it all together.
4. Add turmeric, sugar, curry powder, chillies, cumin and coriander. Cook for a few minutes.
5. Add the coconut milk and bring to the boil. Simmer for about 10 minutes. Stir occasionally.
6. Add the mutton and simmer for an hour. The meat should be tender.
7. Add salt and pepper.
8. Cut the loaf of bread in half and hollow out both halves. Make sure you do not take out too much bread, so the crust is thick enough to hold the curry mixture.
9. Place the curry mix in the bread and make a lid with the bread you hollowed out. Use this lid to scoop up the curry sauce.
10. This is a messy business, but it tastes lovely!

38

7.8 VEGETARIAN BUNNY CHOW

Ingredients
1 loaf of bread cut in half.
1 cup kidney beans
3 cups of water with a vegetable stock cube
1 cup sugar beans
2 grated carrots
2 potatoes cut in cubes
2 onions
1 clove of garlic
Oil
1 tablespoon curry powder (mild or hot, to your taste)
1 teaspoon cinnamon
1 teaspoon turmeric
1 teaspoon thyme
Salt and pepper

Method
1. Boil kidney beans in the stock and water for about 20 minutes and then add the sugar beans, carrots and potatoes (cut in cubes).
2. Boil for another 50 minutes.
3. Fry the onion and garlic in the oil.
4. Add the curry, cinnamon, turmeric and thyme. Stir for about 2 minutes.
5. Mix the onion and beans all together, adding the salt and pepper as well. Let this mixture boil until the potatoes are soft.
6. Thicken the gravy if so required.
7. Place the curry in the hollowed out half loaf of bread. Use the bread you hollowed out to soak up the lovely sauce.

7.9 GREAT CURRY

Ingredients
1kg lamb rib (cut off the excess fat and cube the meat. You can use beef.)
2 chopped onions
Sunflower oil (to fry onions in)
1 ½ cups water with 2 meat stock cubes
1 teaspoon coriander
1 teaspoon cinnamon
2 cloves crushed garlic
1 tablespoon curry powder
1 teaspoon turmeric
1 tablespoon cornflour (mix with a little bit of water)
4 potatoes cut in little cubes
2 tomatoes
5 dried, chopped apricots or ¼ cup of fruit chutney
Salt and pepper
1 teaspoon lemon juice

Method
1. Sauté the onions in the oil until it is light brown.
2. Add the water and stock cubes, coriander, cinnamon, garlic, curry and turmeric and simmer for a few minutes. Stir constantly.
3. Add the meat and the rest of the ingredients. Simmer for an hour (over a low heat), making sure you stir often and that there is enough water.
4. Serve with yellow rice, sliced banana, desiccated coconut and chutney.

PS: you can add vegetables if you like, or just serve it on the side.

7.10 HISTORY OF "POTJIEKOS"

"Potjiekos" has been part of our lives for many centuries. Food used to be cooked in an open hearth in the kitchen. The Dutch used a cast iron pot with legs so coals could be scraped underneath the pot. The all in one meal, *"potjiekos",* was born when easy cooking became a necessity to the "Voortrekkers". They made this their own by adding any vegetables and meat they could find so they could keep body and soul together.

They would add all the ingredients, hang the pot underneath the wagon in the morning and cooking it when they arrived in the evening outside over the open fire. Coals are placed underneath the pot and the lid is kept tightly closed so the natural juices of the food can create a lovely, rich gravy.

The *"potjies"* (pots) come in many different sizes. These sizes depend on the amount of fluid it holds. A number 1 potjie holds 2 quarts of water while the number 3 potjie holds 8 quarts. The size makes a difference when it comes to how many people you are cooking for.

Today everybody has their own secret ingredients. This style of cooking has become so popular in South Africa that various *"potjiekos"* competitions are held every year all around the country. The greatest recipes appear from these competitions and they are then shown on television cooking programmes.

If you don't have a "potjie", don't let this stop you from trying a great way of cooking. Use a heavy based sauce pan or pot with a close fitting lid and create a passable version. But there's nothing as great as the real thing.

There are as many "potjiekos" recipes as there are people in our beautiful country. Anything from chicken, beef, lamb, prawns, seafood and many more. The reason I chose the chicken recipe, is because this is my favourite!

7.10.1 "POTJIEKOS"

Ingredients

About 2kg chicken pieces
2 onions
2 green peppers
Oil
4 cups water
Salt and pepper
1 teaspoon thyme
1 teaspoon coriander
1 teaspoon cloves

Vegetables: Baby potatoes with the skin
Mushrooms
Baby marrows
Carrots
Little gem squash
Yellow and green pattiepans
Green beans
Chicken casserole
½ cup semi-sweet wine

Method

1. Fry the onion and green pepper in the oil. Remove the onions and fry the chicken in the same oil until light brown. Season with salt, pepper, thyme, coriander and cloves.
2. Add the onions back in with 2 cups of water, close the lid and leave for 2 hours. Stir the meat every ½ an hour.
3. Add the potatoes first and leave for about 30 minutes to an hour. Stir the chicken before you add the vegetables and another cup of water.
4. Make sure you close the lid tightly. It is very important not to stir the food after this.
5. When the vegetables are cooked, in about 1 ½ hour (if the vegetables are not soft enough, leave for another ½ hour), mix some chicken casserole with ½ a cup of water and ½ a cup of white wine. Add to the *"potjie"*.
6. Leave the *"potjie"* for another 15 minutes.
7. Serve the *"potjiekos"* with rice and salad (salad recipes can be found under the heading "salads").

7.11 WATER LILY STEW ("Waterblommetjiebredie")

A *"bredie"* is soul food for us all. It can be described as a rich, slow-cooked stew with a variety of spices.   The *"bredie"* is usually made with tomatoes or "waterblommetjies" (water lilies, little water flowers).   This is a perfect combination of vegetables and meat cooked for a very long time. The meat has a beautiful vegetable flavour while the vegetables benefit from the fluids of the meat.

Ingredients
2 ½ bundles of water lilies
1 ½ kg lamb
1 teaspoon salt
½ teaspoon pepper
2 onions, cut in rings
1 sour apple, cut up in slices
1 cup water
1 cup white wine
2 potatoes

Method
1. Wash the flowers, let it soak in salt water and cut off the stems.
2. Place the meat in a pot with salt and pepper and fry until brown.
3. Fry the onions in the fat of the meat.
4. Mix all the ingredients, including the potatoes that are cut up.
5. Let the meat simmer for about an hour, until soft. Do not stir unnecessarily.
6. Serve with boiled rice and vegetables. It also goes very well with a green salad.

7.12 TOMATO STEW ("Tamatiebredie")

Ingredients
2 onions
2 crushed cloves of garlic
A bit of sunflower oil
1 teaspoon cinnamon
1 teaspoon ginger
3 cardamon seeds
1 ½ kg mutton
1 cup water
2 teaspoons salt
Pepper
1 chilli, chopped
8 tomatoes (skinned and chopped)
4 potatoes (cut in cubes)
2 tablespoons of sugar
1 teaspoon dried thyme
1 tablespoon butter
1 tablespoon flour

Method
1. Sauté onions in the oil together with the garlic.
2. Add the cinnamon, ginger and cardamon seeds.
3. Mix the meat and the onions together with one cup of water.
4. Add the salt, pepper and chilli.
5. Place the lid on the pot and let it simmer for 1 hour.
6. Add the tomatoes, potatoes, sugar and thyme. Let it simmer for another hour.
7. Mix the melted butter with 1 tablespoon of flour. Add this to the mixture to thicken the *"bredie"*.

Serve with boiled rice and vegetables.

7.13 CHAKALAKA

Ingredients
2 onions
2 chilli peppers
2 sweet peppers
5 grated carrots
Oil
1 teaspoon ground garlic
1 teaspoon ginger
2 tablespoons curry powder
400g tinned baked beans in tomato sauce
Salt and pepper

Method
1. Fry the onions, chillies, sweet peppers and grated carrots in oil for 8 minutes while stirring.
2. Add the garlic, ginger, curry powder and baked beans in tomato sauce.
3. Mix well and simmer for about 10 minutes
4. Add the salt and pepper and let it cool down.
5. Serve at room temperature on it's own, or with rice.

7.14 DRIED MEAT

In South Africa it is absolutely unthinkable to watch a great rugby or cricket match without some "biltong" or *"droë wors"* (dried sausage). This goes very well together with beer, *"braai"* and rugby. Today no South African can even stand the thought of not being able to eat either!

There are two very famous types of dried meat. *"Biltong"* is the first type. It is dried meat, known to be a favourite of South Africans for over 400 years. This was a great idea to preserve meat in the past because the *"Voortrekkers"* were constantly moving around. They made this great delicacy by using any meat that was available, making it as they were travelling. Strips of meat are rubbed with spices and vinegar, which was the only way to keep the meat fresh in a very warm climate.

Dried sausage is the second type and another form of *"biltong"*. This is dried meat that it put into casings. The Voortrekkers would make a lot of *"boerewors"* at a time while they stopped over to rest. No food would be wasted, therefore they had to make a plan to preserve these meats. The *"wors"* (sausages) that were left over would be hung up to dry. The easiest way to do this, was to put the sausage under the ox wagons or wherever they could find space.

7.14.1 "BILTONG"

Ingredients
1kg meat (can be any meat including ostrich and beef)
1 cup vinegar
½ cup brown sugar
½ cup coriander
1 teaspoon pepper
3 tablespoons salt
1 tablespoon bicarbonate of soda
2 teaspoons saltpetre
4 cups of water
String

Method
1. Wash the meat and then cut it against the grain into strips of about one inch.
2. Sprinkle a little bit of vinegar on the meat.
3. Mix the sugar, coriander, pepper, salt, bicarbonate of soda and saltpetre. Rub this mixture into the meat.
4. Place the meat in a tray and leave it in the fridge for about 24 hours.
5. Dump the blood that seeped out of the meat.
6. Mix the water and vinegar together and dip the meat quickly in the mix.
7. Tap the meat dry and hang it up.
8. Make sure when you hang it up that you use S-shaped hooks that you place at the top end of the meat. Hang the meat up in a cool light place. You can use a fan and electric light to create the best situation. Leave the meat hanging for 1 to 3 weeks, depending on how dry you would like the "biltong" to be.

7.14.2   DRIED SAUSAGE ("Droë wors")

Ingredients
2kg venison
1kg beef
500g sheep tails fat (do not use pork fat)
½ cup brown vinegar
2 tablespoons brandy (this is optional)
2 tablespoons salt
1 teaspoon pepper
1 tablespoon coriander
½ teaspoon ground cloves
200g of narrow sausage casing

Method
1. Mix the meat and the fat together and put it through a mincer.
2. Mix the rest together and add it to the meat. Mix lightly.
3. Place it in the refrigerator for about 3 hours so the spices can mix with the meat.
4. Soak the casing in water while the meat is in the refrigerator. Make sure the casings are not overstuffed.
5. Dry the sausage by hanging it up with S-shaped hooks in a dry place. Let it dry for about a week.
6. Once it is dry the sausage should snap easily.

8. Side Dishes

Side dishes complete the main courses: It complements the main dish and the presentation is beautiful. The following recipes go very well with almost anything. Try it!

8.1 YELLOW RICE

Yellow rice is usually served with either *"bobotie"* (recipe can be found under the heading, **Main Dishes**) or any curry meal. Add banana and coconut when eating curry dishes as it complements it very well.

Ingredients
1 cup rice
3 cups water
Salt and pepper
1 teaspoon turmeric
½ teaspoon cinnamon
½ cup raisins

Method
1. Wash the rice.
2. Boil the water and add all the ingredients, except for the raisins.
3. Boil the rice for 10 minutes.
4. Drain the water, add the raisins and steam for about 2 minutes.

8.2 BILTONG AND CHEESE POT BREAD

Ingredients
8 cups of flour
1 tablespoon salt
1 tablespoon sugar
1 packet of instant bread yeast
2 tablespoons of butter/margarine
1 cup *"biltong"*
1 cup grated cheese
Water
1 beaten egg

Method
1. Sieve the flour and salt together. Add the sugar and yeast.
2. Rub the margarine in with the flour mix using your fingertips.
3. Add the "biltong" and the grated cheese.
4. Add luke-warm water to the mixture (start with about ½ cup), to make sure the dough can be handled.
5. Knead the dough for about 10 minutes and make sure the dough is elastic.
6. Place the dough in a bag and leave it to stand for 20 minutes.
7. Knead the dough down and form it in a ball.
8. Place the dough in a bowl and cover it with a bag. Let it stand for 20 more minutes and let it rise to twice the size.
9. Beat the egg and smear it on the dough.
10. Bake for 45 minutes in a pre-heated oven at 200°C (or bake it in a *pot* – looks like a *"potjie"* for "potjiekos").

8.3 POTATO CAKES

Ingredients
2 cups of mashed potato
1 tablespoon butter
Salt and pepper
2 eggs

Method
1. Mix the butter, salt and pepper with the potatoes.
2. Add the egg yolks to the potatoes and mix.
3. Beat the white of the eggs very well and fold into the mixture.
4. Smear a pan with a little bit of butter and place spoons full of the mixture on the pan.
5. Bake the potato cakes in a pre-heated oven at 180°C for about 10 minutes, or until the potato cakes are light brown.

8.4 CINNAMON DUMPLINGS ("Souskluitjies")

Ingredients
1 cup flour
Pinch of salt
½ teaspoon ginger
1 teaspoon cinnamon
1 teaspoon bicarbonate of soda
1 tablespoon butter
1 egg
1 tablespoon apricot jam

Method
1. Sieve flour, salt, ginger, cinnamon and bicarbonate of soda together.
2. Add the butter and use your fingers to rub into the mixture.
3. Add 1 beaten egg and apricot jam.
4. Mix together.

Syrup
3 ½ cups water
1 cup sugar
Little bit of lemon juice or vinegar.

1. Mix together and let it come to the boil.
2. Place spoons full of dough in the syrup mix
3. Boil for 20 minutes, leaving the lid on.

8.5 POTATO "MIELIE" DISH

Ingredients
4 potatoes
2 teaspoons aromat
Salt and pepper
6 strips of bacon
1 chopped onion
1 tin of sweet corn
1 cup grated cheese
2 eggs
A splash of Tabasco sauce
1 cup of cream

Method
1. Boil the potatoes until almost soft. Sprinkle the aromat, salt and pepper over.
2. Grill the bacon and cut into little pieces. Mix it with the onion.
3. Slice halve the potatoes and place them in a bowl.
4. Place some of the onion and bacon on top of this layer of potatoes.
5. Empty half a tin of the sweet corn on top.
6. Add half of the grated cheese.
7. Repeat number 3 to 6 above.
8. Mix the eggs, Tabasco sauce and cream together.
9. Pour over the potatoes and bake for about 30 minutes in a pre-heated oven at 180°C.

8.6   CREAM SPINACH

Ingredients
3 cups of spinach
2 tablespoons butter
½ teaspoon garlic
½ onion
2 tablespoons flour
1 cup of cream

Method
1. Boil the spinach in water until soft. Make sure it is VERY dry before chopping the spinach very thinly.
2. Melt the butter and add the garlic and onion. When the onion is light brown, add the flour.
3. Add the cream very slowly and mix. Make sure there are no lumps.
4. Add the spinach to the sauce and mix well.
5. Serve warm.

8.7 WARM POTATO DISH

Ingredients
6 potatoes
1 onion, chopped
6 slices of bacon
1 teaspoon garlic flakes
2 green peppers
1 cup of cream
2 tablespoons butter
1 packet of thick white onion soup
Salt and pepper
Grated cheese

Method
1. Cut potatoes in rings and boil until soft.
2. Sauté the onion, bacon, garlic and green pepper. Keep separate.
3. Mix the cream, melted butter and onion soup together.
4. Place one layer of potatoes in a bowl, season with salt and pepper, add ½ the onion mix and ½ of the cream mixture on top.
5. Repeat this again with the other half that is left.
6. Sprinkle grated cheese on top of the cream.
7. Bake in a pre-heated oven at 180 °C for 20 minutes.

8.8 SWEET POTATO IN SAUCE

Ingredients
3 cups of fresh, raw, sweet potatoes, peeled and cut in rings
Water
½ cup brown sugar
1 tablespoon butter/margarine

Method
1. Boil the sweet potatoes in water, just enough to cover them. Also add the sugar. Boil until soft.
2. When the sweet potatoes are almost ready, add the butter and boil for another minute.
3. Mash the sweet potatoes with a fork (you can leave the sweet potatoes in rings) and serve as a side dish to any meat.
4. Sugar quantity can vary depending on your taste.

8.9 PUMPKIN AND MUSHROOM DISH

Ingredients
1 tablespoon butter
1 diced onion
1 cup of mushrooms
1 butternut squash, pealed and cut into thin cubes
750g baby marrow
1 packet of thick white onion soup
1 cup of cream

Method
1. Fry the onions in the butter and add the mushrooms.
2. Place the pumpkin and the mushrooms in layers in a bowl.
3. Sprinkle the onion soup on the top.
4. Pour the cream over the top and cover the bowl with either a lid or foil.
5. Bake in a pre-heated over at 180°C for 1 hour.

8.10 SALTED YELLOW CARROTS

Ingredients
5 carrots
1 large potato
½ onion (finely chopped)
Salt and pepper
1 tablespoon butter

Method
1. Peel the carrots and potato and cut them into little circles.
2. Finely chop the onion.
3. Bring a cup of water to the boil and add the carrots, potato and onion.
4. When it is almost ready (between 10 and 15 minutes), add the salt, pepper and butter.
5. Boil for a few more minutes until the carrots are soft and the water boiled away. Mash together.

8.11 PUMPKIN CAKES ("Pampoenkoekies")

Pumpkin flavoured with cinnamon is one of our most favourite vegetables and varieties include "boere" pumpkin, butternut squash, herbert squash, red pumpkin, gem squash and more. To make *"pampoenkoekies"*, the best choice will be herbert squash or red pumpkin. Living in London, different types of pumpkin are not readily available, so I have experimented with butternut squash. This is available in most stores.

Ingredients
2 cups of pumpkin (1 medium-sized butternut squash)   Salt
4 tablespoons flour   1 egg
2 teaspoons baking powder   Sunflower oil

Method
1. Boil the pumpkin in a little bit of water until soft (between 10 and 15 minutes). Make sure the pumpkin is very dry before using. Mash the pumpkin.
2. Add the flour, baking powder, salt and egg. Mix well.
3. Warm up a little bit of oil in a frying pan. Place spoons full in the pan and fry on both sides until golden brown.
4. *"Pampoenkoekies"* can be served with cinnamon sugar (cinnamon mixed with sugar) or a sweet syrup.

Syrup
1 tablespoon butter/margarine   1 ½ cups sugar
¾ cup water   1 tablespoon cornflour
¾ cup milk

1. Bring the butter, water, milk and sugar to the boil.
2. Mix cornflour with a little bit of water and add. Let it boil for about 2 minutes.
3. Pour warm syrup over the *"pampoenkoekies"* (instead of cinnamon sugar).

9. Salads

Salads are high on our priority list. The reason is very easy and straight forward. The climate of South Africa gives us the perfect opportunity to experiment with all fruits and vegetables.

Serving food cold is very pleasant on a warm afternoon. Therefore salads are a very important part of our lives. There is nothing nicer than a *"braaivleis"* served with cold salads, freshly made from the fridge on a hot summers Saturday afternoon.

9.1 SNOEK SALAD (FISH)

Ingredients
2 onions
1 tablespoon butter/margarine
2 cups snoek (or fish of your choice)
Salt and pepper
1 tablespoon of sugar
½ cup of vinegar
¼ cup of cream

Method
1. Fry the chopped onion in a tablespoon of butter.
2. Add the rest of the ingredients, except for the cream, and let it boil.
3. Remove from stove. Add the cream and mix.

9.2 TUNA NOODLE SALAD

Ingredients
1 packet of shell noodles
1 tin of peaches (drain the sauce)
1 tin of tuna
1 cup of mayonnaise (can use more or less, depending on taste)

Method
1. Boil the noodles and let it cool down.
2. Cut the peaches finely and add to the noodles. Also add the tuna.
3. Lastly, add the mayonnaise and mix very well.
4. Place in the refrigerator and serve chilled.

PS: If you do not like tuna, you can leave it out. The noodles with peaches and mayonnaise taste lovely on its own.

9.3 CURRY NOODLE SALAD

Ingredients
1 packet of screw noodles
1 chopped onion
1 green pepper, chopped
½ cup raisins
1 tin of finely cut peaches

1. Boil the noodles in water. Make sure it's not too soft. Let it cool down.
2. Add the chopped onion, green pepper, raisins and peaches. Mix together

Sauce
1 ½ teaspoons mild curry powder
½ cup mayonnaise
¼ cup chutney
Salt and pepper

1. Mix all the ingredients for the sauce together.
2. Add to the noodles and mix well.
3. Place in refrigerator and let it cool down for about 5 hours. Serve cold.

9.4 CHICKEN AND AVOCADO SALAD

Ingredients
2 chicken breasts
½ lettuce
10 thinly sliced slices of cucumber
8 cocktail tomatoes cut in half
1 onion (cut in rings)
1 avocado
Feta Cheese

Method
1. Grill the chicken and let it cool down.
2. Break the lettuce with your fingers and place in the bottom of the bowl.
3. Add the cucumber and tomatoes for colour.
4. Place the onion rings on top of this.
5. Cut the chicken breasts into strips and place on top of the onions.
6. Cut the avocado in slices and place on top of the chicken. Cube the feta cheese and place on top of the avocado.
7. Make an easy salad dressing by mixing olive oil, a pinch of sugar and a bit of vinegar.

9.5   POTATO SALAD

Ingredients
6 potatoes
Salt and pepper
2 tablespoons grated raw onion
1 teaspoon parsley
Mayonnaise
2 hard boiled eggs

Method
1.   Boil the potatoes in their skin. Let it cool down and remove the skin.
2.   Cut the potatoes into little cubes and add the salt, pepper, onion and parsley.
3.   Add the mayonnaise and mix well.
4.   Slice the eggs and place on top of the salad.
5.   Leave in the refrigerator for about 5 hours. Serve cold.

9.6   BEETROOT SALAD

Ingredients
3 bushes of beetroot (about 15) – this is a big quantity to bottle them and use later. You can make only half if you want a smaller quantity.

Sauce
2 cups water
2 cups white vinegar
2 cups sugar
½ teaspoon salt
½ teaspoon fine cloves
½ teaspoon black pepper
½ teaspoon fine ginger

Method
1.   Boil the beetroot in water until soft. Test if the beetroot is ready in the same way you would check potatoes.
2.   Remove the skin of the beetroot and grate.
3.   Add all the ingredients for the sauce in a bowl and bring to the boil.
4.   Add the beetroot to the sauce and simmer for 20 minutes.
5.   Remove from stove and place warm in bottles if you would like to store it for a while.
6.   If you want to eat, just place in the refrigerator for a day and enjoy cold.

9.7   THREE BEAN SALAD

Ingredients for salad
1 tin French cut green beans
1 tin Butter beans
1 tin Baked beans in tomato sauce
1 green pepper
½ chopped onion
½ cup sultanas

1. Mix all the ingredients together.

Marinade
½ cup brown sugar
1 ½ tablespoons cornflour
2 tablespoons sunflower oil
¾ cup white vinegar
1 teaspoon mustard powder

Method
1.   Mix all of the above ingredients for the marinade together and boil until it thickens.
2.   Add the beans to the sauce and mix well.

9.8 PEA SALAD

Ingredients
1 celery stick
½ lettuce
½ bag of frozen peas
½ tin condensed milk
¼ cup mayonnaise

Method
1. Chop the celery and lettuce.
2. Mix all of the above ingredients together.
3. Salad must be served cold (add more condensed milk if necessary).

9.9 CURRY CARROT SALAD

Ingredients
6 yellow carrots
Salt
1 green pepper
1 ½ onions

1. Cut the carrots into circles and boil until almost soft in salted water.
2. Cut the green pepper into little pieces and the onions into rings. Add to the carrots and mix.

Sauce
1 packet tomato soup
1 cup water
½ cup vinegar
¼ cup oil
½ cup sugar
1 teaspoon mustard powder
Salt and pepper

1. Mix all of the above ingredients for the sauce and bring to the boil.
2. Stir and let boil for about 2 minutes.
3. Add the warm sauce over the carrot mix and let it cool down.
4. Refrigerate for about 1 day and serve cold.

9.10 CARROT AND PINEAPPLE SALAD

This must be the easiest salad you can ever make! It tastes great, is refreshing and quick to make!

Ingredients
6 finely grated carrots
1 tin of crushed pineapple

Method
1. Mix the grated carrots and pineapple together and place in the refrigerator.
2. Serve cold and enjoy!

9.11 FRUIT BOAT SALAD

Ingredients
1 watermelon
1 green melon
1 orange melon (honey sweet)
1 paw-paw
2 bunches of black grapes
2 bunches of green grapes
12 lychees

Method
1. Cut all the fruit in half, except for the grapes and lychees.
2. Use a little round scoop, and make balls from all the fruit.
3. Use one half of the hollowed out watermelon as the salad bowl and add all the fruit together.

PS: This fruit salad can be served as part of a main course (or even a "braai") and also as a dessert. Serve the fruit salad with cream or ice cream.

9.12 GREEN MIXED SALAD

Ingredients
1 lettuce
3 tomatoes
½ onion
1 small cucumber
1 fresh pineapple
1 avocado
1 cup of feta cheese

Method
1. Rinse the lettuce and break the leaves.
2. Cut the tomatoes into little squares. (Cocktail tomatoes can also be used)
3. The onion and cucumber need to be cut in rings.
4. Pineapple, avocado and feta cheese to be cut into little squares.
5. Add all the ingredients in the same order as the ingredients are listed. Mix the salad.

Add a Greek salad dressing if it is to your taste.

9.13 BANANA SALAD

Ingredients
8 bananas
½ cup lemon juice
½ cup chopped peanuts
3 tablespoons mayonnaise
¼ cup condensed milk (can use more if it isn't sweet enough)
¼ teaspoon mustard powder

Method
1. Cut the bananas in circle form.
2. Role the bananas in the lemon juice and then in the peanuts.
3. Mix the mayonnaise, condensed milk and mustard powder together.
4. Add to the bananas.

PS: 1 teaspoon of curry powder can be added instead of mustard as variation to the recipe.

10. Sauces

10.1 MONKEY GLAND SAUCE

Monkey gland sauce should be tried with any grilled steak!

Ingredients
2 onions
2 sliced cloves of garlic
1 teaspoon ginger
1 tablespoon sunflower oil
½ cup water
1 teaspoon Tabasco sauce
½ cup tomato sauce
½ cup fruit chutney
¼ cup tomato paste
1 tablespoon honey
½ cup brown sugar
Salt and black pepper
¼ cup port

Method
1. Sauté the onions, garlic and ginger in the oil.
2. Add the rest of the ingredients and simmer over a low heat for 15 minutes.
3. Serve warm with steaks and even chicken.

10.2 SWEET AND SOUR SAUCE

Ingredients
½ onion
1 large tin of chopped tomatoes
Small tin of pineapple pieces
¼ cup tomato paste
1 teaspoon ginger
2 tablespoons brown sugar
1 ½ tablespoons vinegar
Salt and pepper
½ teaspoon mixed herbs
1 tablespoon cornflour

Method
1. Chop the onion very thinly and sauté in a little oil until soft.
2. Add the tin of tomatoes and the rest of the ingredients, except for the cornflour. (Pour the sauce from the pineapple in as well). Bring to the boil.
3. Mix the cornflour with a little bit of water and add to the rest.
4. Stir and let simmer for about 3 minutes.

10.3 BASIC WHITE SAUCE

Ingredients
1 cup low fat milk
1 ½ tablespoons cornflour
Pinch of salt
Red pepper
Paprika

Method
1. Pour the milk in a saucepan and bring to the boil.
2. Mix the cornflour with a little bit of milk and add to the boiling milk. Stir well.
3. Add the salt, pepper and paprika and mix until the sauce is thick and creamy.

PS: This is a quick and easy sauce. If you want a more traditional sauce, use the following recipe:

Ingredients
1 ½ tablespoons butter
2 tablespoons flour
Pinch of salt and pepper
1 ¼ cups of milk (use more milk if you want the sauce to be thinner)

Method
1. Melt the butter and add the flour, salt and pepper.
2. Add the milk a little at a time, keep stirring and make sure the sauce is smooth and without any lumps.

10.4 CHEESE AND ONION SAUCE

Ingredients
1 cup milk
½ cup cream
Pinch of salt and pepper
Pinch of paprika
½ packet of thick white onion soup
½ cup cheese
1 tablespoon cornflour

Method
1. Boil the milk and add the cream, salt, pepper, paprika, onion soup and cheese.
2. Mix the cornflour with a little bit of water and add to the sauce.
3. Stir until the sauce becomes thicker.

10.5 MUSHROOM AND CHEESE SAUCE

Ingredients
1 ½ tablespoons butter/margarine
2 tablespoons flour
Salt and pepper
1 ¼ cups milk (depending on how thick you want the sauce)
½ cup of grated cheese
6 mushrooms

Method
1. Melt the butter and add the flour, salt and pepper. Mix well.
2. Add the milk slowly (a little bit at a time) and stir very well. Make sure there are no lumps in the sauce.
3. Add the cheese and the finely chopped mushrooms. Stir for about 2 minutes.

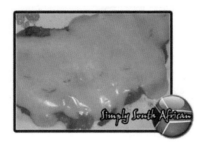

10.6 PERI-PERI SAUCE

Ingredients
2 tablespoons white vinegar
2 tablespoons oil
2 teaspoons Worcestershire sauce
2 teaspoons paprika
1 teaspoon mustard powder
1 teaspoon peri-peri
2 cloves of garlic
Salt and aromat
1 green or red chilli, chopped

Method
1.   Mix all of the ingredients together and boil for about 3 minutes.

PS: This is a very hot sauce and is especially great with chicken wings. If you prefer a sauce that is not too hot, use the green chilli, rather than the red one.

10.7 BAR ONE SAUCE (MARS BAR SAUCE)

Ingredients
3 Bar One bars (you can use Mars Bars if you do not have a Bar One)
1 tin (397g) of condensed milk
1 cup of cream
1 teaspoon of vanilla extract

Method
1.   Melt the Bar Ones' in the condensed milk.
2.   Remove the above from the heat and mix the cream and vanilla essence with the mixture.
3.   Serve warm over your favourite ice cream. This is a very sweet sauce but great for those of you with a sweet tooth!

10.8 WINE SAUCE

This is a great recipe that goes very nicely with a cottage pudding. This recipe can be found under the heading, **Warm Desserts**.

Ingredients
½ cup sugar
2 cups water
Skin of ½ an orange
Pinch of salt
1 teaspoon butter/margarine
1 teaspoon cornflour
½ cup semi-sweet wine
1 tablespoon apricot jam

Method
1. Boil the sugar, water, skin of ½ an orange and salt together for 5 minutes.
2. Add the butter.
3. Thicken the sauce with cornflour, mixed with a little bit of water.
4. Add the wine and apricot jam and boil for another 4 minutes.
5. Serve hot over your dessert.

11. Warm Desserts

11.1 SAGO PUDDING

Ingredients
1 ½ cups sago
3 cups water
2 cups milk
½ teaspoon salt
1 tin (397g) condensed milk
3 beaten eggs
1 tablespoon butter
1 teaspoon vanilla extract

Method
1. Mix the sago, water, milk and salt in a bowl.
2. Place this in the microwave on high for 3 minutes. Make sure you mix after every minute.
3. Place back in the microwave for another 10 - 12 minutes until the sago is see-through.
4. Add the rest of the ingredients, and mix very well.

11.2 BREAD PUDDING (South African version)

Ingredients
2 cups breadcrumbs
2 cups milk
2 eggs
½ cup sugar
2 teaspoons grated orange skin
½ cup butter
1 teaspoon vanilla extract
¼ cup boiling water
Apricot jam

Method
1. Soak the breadcrumbs in the milk.
2. Beat 1 of the eggs with half the sugar, orange skin and half the melted butter. Pour over the breadcrumbs.
3. Bake in a pre-heated oven at 180°C for 30 minutes.
4. Mix the rest of the butter, sugar, vanilla, 1 egg and boiling water together (the sauce).
5. Spread apricot jam on top of the warm dessert, then pour the sauce over the top and bake in the oven for another 20 minutes until brown.

Desserts have always been a big favourite. The biggest influence came from the British that arrived in South Africa in the 1700's. Some are old English favourites, and some new ideas gave birth to original South African recipes. You will find both traditional South African recipes, as well as other old favourites.

11.3 BREAD AND BUTTER PUDDING

Ingredients
10 slices of white bread, with the crusts cut off
½ cup sugar
2 tablespoons butter
4 cups milk
4 eggs

Method
1. Smear the 10 slices of bread with butter and place in an ovenproof bowl. Make sure you smear the bowl with butter first. Sprinkle the sugar on top.
2. Melt 2 tablespoons of butter in the milk.
3. Beat the eggs very well and add to the milk mixture. Mix.
4. Pour over the bread and let it stand for a few minutes before baking it in a pre-heated oven at 180°C for about 30 minutes.

Top layer
1 cup butter
1 ¾ cups sugar
2 eggs
2 teaspoons vanilla extract

Method
1. Cream the butter and sugar together.
2. Add the eggs, one at a time.
3. Add the vanilla and mix until there are no lumps.
4. When the pudding is removed from the oven after 30 minutes, smear this mixture on top and place back in the oven very quickly.
5. Bake for a further 20 minutes.
6. Serve with custard.

11.4 COTTAGE PUDDING

Ingredients
½ cup butter/margarine

1 cup sugar

2 eggs

2 cups flour

2 teaspoons baking powder

Pinch of salt

1 cup milk

Method
1. Cream the butter and sugar together. Beat the eggs and add.
2. Sieve the flour, baking powder and salt and add to the butter mixture.
3. Add milk slowly and mix.
4. Place in a round pan and bake in a pre-heated oven at 180°C for 45 minutes to 1 hour.

Wine sauce Ingredients
½ cup sugar

2 cups water

Pinch of salt

Skin of ½ an orange

1 teaspoon butter/margarine

1 teaspoon cornflour

½ cup semi-sweet wine

1 tablespoon apricot jam

Method
1. Boil the sugar, water, salt and orange skin together for 5 minutes. Add the butter.
2. Thicken the sauce with cornflour, mixed with a little bit of water.
3. Add the wine and apricot jam. Boil for about another 2 minutes.
4. Serve the sauce hot and pour over the warm cottage pudding. Add custard to enhance the flavour. Make sure it is served hot. Enjoy.

11.5 ROLY POLY (serves 4, but recipe can be doubled)

Ingredients

1 cup flour
2 tablespoons margarine/butter
2 teaspoons baking powder
Salt

1 egg
¼ cup milk
Apricot jam

Method
1. Rub the flour, butter, baking powder and salt with your fingertips.
2. Beat the egg and mix with a little (about ¼ cup) bit of milk. Mix with the rest.
3. Roll out the dough and smear apricot jam on the top.
4. Roll up the dough and place in a bowl.

Sauce

¾ cup water
¾ cup sugar
1 tablespoon butter

1. Boil the water, sugar and butter together and add the sauce in the same bowl as the dough.
2. Bake in a pre-heated oven at 180°C for about 25 minutes.

11.6 LEAP YEAR PUDDING

Ingredients

3 tablespoons butter
½ cup sugar
1 cup flour
2 teaspoons baking powder
Pinch of salt

2 eggs
1 ¼ cups milk (must be cold)
1 tablespoon sugar
2 tablespoons apricot jam

Method
1. Mix the butter, sugar, flour, baking powder, salt and the egg yolks together with about a ¼ cup of milk.
2. Place in a pan and bake in a pre-heated oven at 180°C for about 30 minutes.
3. Beat the white of the eggs together with one tablespoon of sugar until thick.
4. Pour the cup of cold milk over the warm dessert. Then smear the apricot jam on top and place the egg white on top of the jam.
5. Place back in the oven and bake for another 10 minutes, or until the egg white on top is light brown.

11.7 "DOEK" PUDDING

Ingredients
1 cup butter
1 ¼ cups sugar
3 eggs
1 teaspoon bicarbonate of soda
½ cup boiling water
2 tablespoons apricot jam
2 tablespoons orange skin (zest of orange)
1 cup breadcrumbs
1 teaspoon cinnamon
1 teaspoon fine ginger
3 cups flour
Pinch of salt
1 teaspoon fine nuts
1 cup dates
1 cup raisins
1 cup sultanas
1 cup currents

Method
1. Cream the butter and sugar together.
2. Add the eggs one at a time and mix.
3. Mix the bicarbonate of soda with the boiling water and add together with the jam, breadcrumbs, orange skin and spices.
4. Sieve the flour and salt and add.
5. Lastly add the fruit and make sure the mixture is quite thick.
6. Take a clean linen cloth or pillowcase and sprinkle with flour. Place the mixture into the cloth and tie it up.
7. Place in a large saucepan with about ¾ full of boiling water. Place a lid on top of the pan and steam for 3 hours. If the water gets low, add more boiling water, but only lift the lid half way. Try not to open unless absolutely necessary.

Butter sauce
2 cups sugar
1 cup water
1 cup butter
2 beaten eggs
2 teaspoons cinnamon

1. Mix all the ingredients together and bring to the boil for 5 minutes.
2. Serve warm with the dessert.

11.8 MALVA PUDDING

Ingredients
1 tablespoon butter
1 cup sugar
1 egg
1 cup flour
1 cup milk
Salt
1 teaspoon bicarbonate of soda
1 tablespoon white vinegar
1 tablespoon apricot jam

Method
1. Cream the butter and sugar together.
2. Beat the egg and add with the butter mixture.
3. Add ½ the flour and milk in turn. Add the salt.
4. Mix the bicarbonate of soda and vinegar, then add to the flour mixture.
5. Add the apricot jam lastly and mix.
6. Pour the mixture into an ovenproof dish and bake in a pre-heated oven at 180°C for 25 – 30 minutes.

Sauce
¾ cup sugar
¾ cup milk
1 tablespoon butter
½ cup boiling water

1. Boil all the ingredients together and pour warm over the warm pudding when you take it out of the oven.

11.9 FLOATING ISLAND DESSERT

Ingredients
1 tablespoon butter
½ cup boiling water
1 teaspoon bicarbonate of soda
1 tablespoon golden syrup
1 cup of flour
Pinch of salt
3 tablespoons apricot jam

Method
1. Melt the butter in the boiling water and bicarbonate of soda.
2. Add the rest of the ingredients together with the water mixture.

Sauce
3 cups water
½ cup sugar
1 tablespoon butter
½ teaspoon salt

1. Boil together the ingredients for the sauce and place in a bowl.
2. Drip spoons full of the batter mix in the sauce.
3. Bake in a pre-heated oven at 180°C for about 20 minutes.

12. Cold Desserts

Simply South African

12.1 DOM PEDRO

Ingredients
4 large scoops of ice cream
1 shot of whisky
Little bit of milk
Cream spray gun
Grated chocolate

Method
1. Place the ice cream, whisky and little bit of milk in a bowl and beat well until smooth.
2. Place the mixture in a wineglass.
3. Spray cream on top and sprinkle grated chocolate (or Milo) on top of the cream.

PS: The Dom Pedro can be made with any alcohol of your choice. Mixing the Dom Pedro with a liqueur like Cape Velvet or Amarula, is called an El Pedro.

12.2 YOGHURT PUDDING

Ingredients

2 packets of strawberry jelly
2 cups boiling water
4 cups of custard (Ultra-Mel tastes best)

2 cups strawberry yoghurt
1 cup cream

Method

1. Mix the jelly powder with two cups of boiling water. Let it cool down.
2. Mix the custard and yoghurt together and add to the jelly.
3. Place in refrigerator to cool down.
4. Beat the cream and scoop it on top of the pudding.

12.3 SET PEAR PUDDING

Ingredients

1 tin of (410g) pears
1 cup boiling water

1 packet of lime jelly powder
1 tin (397g) condensed milk

Method

1. Drain the syrup from the pears and cut into little cubes.
2. Add the boiling water to the jelly powder and mix.
3. Add the pears and condensed milk to the jelly.
4. Rinse the round form with water and pour the mixture into the pan.
5. Place in the refrigerator for about 2 hours. Make sure it is set before served
   with either cream or ice cream.

12.4 COOKIE ICE CREAM PUDDING

Ingredients

1 cup cream
1 teaspoon sugar
1 teaspoon vanilla extract
1 packet of chocolate cookies, broken

1 litre of soft vanilla ice cream
1 tin (397g) carnation treat
1 flake

Method

1. Beat the cream, sugar and vanilla extract together.
2. Add the chocolate cookies, ice cream (soft, not melted) and carnation treat
   (or boiled condensed milk). Mix together.
3. Sprinkle flake on top, place in freezable bowl and place in the freezer.

12.5 HOME MADE CHEESECAKE

Ingredients
½ cup condensed milk
1 cup of cottage cheese
2 tablespoons lemon juice
1 cup cream (beaten very well)

Method
1. Mix the condensed milk, cottage cheese and lemon juice together.
2. Add the cream and mix well.

Crust
With the crust, you have 2 choices. Either use a Swiss roll (with apricot jam) or create your own by crumbling 1 packet of plain biscuits and mixing it with ½ cup of melted margarine. Place in a tart board, add the cream cheese mixture on top and place in the refrigerator.

Top layer
1. Pick any fruit you like for example peaches, strawberries or pears. Use 1 tin of your chosen fruit.
2. Put the syrup in a pan and bring to the boil. Add 1 tablespoon of cornflour, mixed with a little bit of water and stir.
3. Let it cool down and pour over the cheesecake.
4. Place the fruit on top of the syrup, place in refrigerator and enjoy it cold with ice cream or maybe cream.

12.6 TRIFLE

There are many variations of the trifle. The one that follows, is the one I grew up with. Whenever you go to the church or school fairs, this is the dessert that you buy. Absolutely lovely! Try it and enjoy every moment.

Ingredients

1 apricot jam Swiss roll
1 large box of custard (Ultra-Mel)
1 big tin of peaches
1 packet of pineapple jelly

1 packet of greengage jelly
1 packet of strawberry jelly
1 bag of crushed nuts

Method
1. Make the jelly, all 3 separate in square bowls and place in the refrigerator the day before you plan to make the trifle.
2. The next day, cut the Swiss roll in slices and place in a square glass holder.
3. Pour the custard on top of the Swiss roll.
4. Cut the peaches into small pieces and place on the custard.
5. Cut all 3 colours jelly into little squares.
6. First place the yellow, then the green and then the red jelly on top of the peaches.
7. Sprinkle the nuts on top (optional).
8. Serve with cream or ice cream.

12.7 CHOCOLATE MOUSSE

Ingredients
3 eggs
1 cup cream
½ cup cocoa
½ cup icing sugar
1/3 slab (50g) of dark chocolate

Method
1. Beat the eggs for about 5 minutes.
2. Beat the cream until thick.
3. Mix the cocoa and icing sugar.
4. Add the eggs and mix very well until smooth.
5. Add the melted chocolate to the mixture.
6. Add the cream lastly and mix very well.
7. Scoop into small wineglasses and place in the refrigerator to set.

12.8 HOME MADE CAPE VELVET

Ingredients
1 tin (397g) condensed milk
1 cup ideal milk
2 eggs
1 teaspoon vanilla extract
1 cup of whiskey (your choice)
1 teaspoon instant coffee powder

Method
1. Mix everything very well together until smooth.
2. Place in refrigerator to cool down.
3. Pour into any container with a cork to store in a cold place until use.

13. Special Treats

13.1 "VETKOEK"

"Vetkoek" is a great tradition. South Africans associate *"vetkoek"* and mince with church and school fairs. *"Vetkoek"* can be enjoyed in 3 great ways. As a main course, a BIG *"vetkoek"* filled with our great curry mince mixture. As a snack with cheese and syrup or as breakfast by dunking it into a cup of tea. *"Vetkoek"* can be enjoyed at any time in any way. A great all-time favourite. It is almost the same consistency as a doughnut.

Ingredients
4 cups flour

1 packet of instant yeast

1 tablespoon butter

1 ¾ cups water

1 tablespoon salt

1 tablespoon honey (optional)

Method
1. Mix the flour and the instant yeast together.
2. Melt the butter with the water and salt. Let the water cool down until luke-warm.
3. Add only a little bit of water at a time and mix.
4. Knead the dough very well. Should be about the same consistency as bread dough.
5. Place it in a bowl with a lid. Cover it with a blanket and make sure it is warm.
6. Leave for at least 2 hours to rise. Take out of the bowl and knead the dough down.
7. Press down with your fingers and cut into blocks.
8. Place oil into a pan and warm up. When the oil is very hot, place the dough into the hot oil and fry on both sides. The *"vetkoek"* is being deep-fried so make sure the pan is filled up with oil.

cut the dough . . .

deep fry . . .

13.2 COCONUT ICE ("Klapperys")

Ingredients
¾ cup water
2 cups sugar
½ teaspoon cream of tartar
Red food colouring
1 ¼ cups desiccated coconut
1 teaspoon vanilla extract

Method
1. Mix the water, sugar and cream of tartar in a sauce pan until the sugar dissolves. Mix very well until it becomes thicker.
2. Remove from the heat and divide the mixture into two separate batches.
3. Place the food colouring and half the coconut in one of the mixtures. Mix very well until creamy and place in a flat baking tray.
4. Add the vanilla and the rest of the coconut to the other part of the mixture. Mix until creamy and place on top of the first mixture.
5. Let it cool down and cut into blocks.

13.3 PANCAKES

Pancakes are enjoyed all over the world with different fillings. Just like *"vetkoek"*, pancakes are also associated with church and school fairs. They are a part of our lives. Nothing beats a cinnamon sugar pancake on a hot or cold day.

You have to go to a South African fare to totally understand this... Even outside shopping centres on Saturday mornings people will stand and bake them on their little portable gas stoves and pans and sell them to everyone walking past. Few people can resist this smell!.

Pancakes around the world are baked in different shapes and thickness. South African pancakes are paper thin and fill the whole size of a frying pan.

Ingredients

2 ½ cups cold water
2 tablespoons oil
3 eggs
1 tablespoon white vinegar

1 ½ cups flour
1 teaspoon baking powder
½ teaspoon salt

Method
1. Beat all the liquids together.
2. Sieve the dry ingredients together and add to the liquid. Beat until smooth.
3. Bake the first pancake in a little bit of oil in a saucepan. Flip it over and brown on both sides.
4. Add cinnamon to sugar and mix. Sprinkle the cinnamon sugar on the pancake and roll up. Enjoy!!

13.4 RAINBOW SANDWICHES

Ingredients

5 slices of bread per person
Butter
Marmite

Biltong cheese spread
Avocado (mashed with a fork)
Tomato sauce

Method
1. Butter the slices of bread.
2. Spread marmite on the first, cheese spread on the second, avocado on the third and tomato sauce on the fourth slice of bread. When you place the slices of bread on top of each other, the spread should be facing up. The fifth slice goes on top.
3. Cut off the crusts and then cut the bread into three fingers.
4. Serve this as a snack before a "braai". Tastes great.

90

13.5 "PLAATKOEKIES" (Like crumpets)

Ingredients
2 eggs
½ cup milk
½ cup water
1 tablespoon sugar
2 cups flour
½ teaspoon salt
4 teaspoons baking powder

Method
1. Beat the eggs with the milk and water (you can substitute the water with just 1 glass of milk if you don't want to use water).
2. Add the rest of the ingredients. Don't stir after the ingredients have been mixed.
3. Let the mixture stand for about 15 minutes before you start baking.
4. Warm up a little bit of oil in a frying pan. Place spoons full of the mixture in the pan.
5. Fry until light brown on both sides (you will know when to flip the cookie over, when air bubbles appear on the top).
6. Serve with butter and add syrup, marmite or cream.

13.6 CINNAMON TOAST

Ingredients
As many slices of bread as you like.
Butter
Cinnamon
Sugar

Method
1. Butter the bread.
2. Mix a bit of cinnamon with sugar and sprinkle on the bread.
3. Place the bread under the grill in the oven until the sugar is melted and the bread light brown around the crusts.

13.7 CHEESE PUFFS

Special treats are exactly what it says: special. Every now and again (sometimes only once a year!) you would get these. Mothers would bake when they had holidays over December with their children. A great way of having fun!

My mother used to bake *"vetkoek"* every Sunday evening and it was the treat of the week. Pancakes are usually baked when it rains, so whenever the rain comes down, you would ask: Mom, are we having pancakes today? It is raining!

Cheese puffs are one of those treats you would get in the evenings, maybe on a Sunday with cheese and cream. It was great!

Ingredients
1 cup flour
2 teaspoons baking powder
½ teaspoon salt
1 cup of grated cheese
1 beaten egg in a cup, filled up to the top with milk

Method
1. Sieve the dry ingredients together.
2. Add the cheese.
3. Lastly, add the cup of egg and milk mixture and mix well.
4. Grease the patty tin and heat the oven to 180°C.
5. Pour into the patty tin and bake for 15 – 20 minutes.
6. Serve hot with butter or margarine.

13.8 MICROWAVE FUDGE

Ingredients
½ cup Rama margarine
1 tin (397g) condensed milk
50g icing sugar (sieved)
1 teaspoon caramel essence

Method
1. Melt the margarine.
2. Add the condensed milk and cook for 2 minutes on high.
3. Add the sieved icing sugar and caramel essence and mix well.
4. Boil for 6 to 8 minutes on high, making sure you stir in between.
5. Remove from the microwave and pour in a glass bowl. Let it cool down and place in the refrigerator. Cut into blocks and serve.

13.9 SCONES

Ingredients
2 cups flour
4 teaspoons baking powder
Pinch of salt
¼ cup butter
¼ - ½ cup milk
1 egg

Method
1. Sieve the dry ingredients together and add the butter. Use your fingertips to rub it in with the flour.
2. Add the rest of the ingredients and mix with a wooden spoon (make sure you don't add too much milk. Only add ¼ at first, it should be enough).
3. Cover the dough with cling film and place in the refrigerator for 15 minutes.
4. Sprinkle the table with flour and place the dough on top. Press lightly and cut in required form.
5. Place on a buttered baking tray and smear a little bit of milk on each scone. Bake in a pre-heated oven at 250°C for about 10 - 15 minutes.
6. Serve with butter and cream, cheese, marmite or apricot jam.

To put another twist on this recipe, add a ½ cup of cheese and cut up 4 viennas and add to the dough. It looks, smells and tastes lovely.

13.10 "YSTERVARKIES"

Ingredients
4 eggs
2 cups sugar
½ cup butter (at room temperature)
½ cup milk
3 cups flour
2 teaspoons baking powder
Pinch of salt
Desiccated coconut

Method
1. Pre-heat the oven to 180°C.
2. Beat the eggs, sugar and butter together until creamy.
3. Add the milk and mix.
4. Sieve the flour, baking powder and salt together.
5. Add to the egg mixture.
6. Place mixture in a baking pan. Make sure you spray the pan so the mixture doesn't stick. (The pan measurements must be as close to the following measurements as possible: 30 cm x 25 cm x 5 cm.)
7. Bake for 1 hour and let it cool down. Cut into blocks of about 4 cm x 4 cm.

Syrup
3 cups sugar
¾ cup cocoa
1 ½ cups water
1 tablespoon butter

1. Mix all the above ingredients (except for the butter) together and bring to the boil. Then add the butter.
2. Turn down the heat and just keep it warm.
3. Take the blocks of cake and dunk it in the syrup. From there, dunk the cake with the syrup into the coconut.
4. Place it in a board or tin that you can close, and leave to cool down before you eat.

13.11 JAM TARTS ("Handtertjies")

Ingredients for puff pastry
2 cups flour
Pinch of salt
1 teaspoon cream of tartar
1 cup butter/margarine
¼ cup ice cold water (use just enough to make the pastry)
Apricot jam

Method
1. Mix flour, salt and cream of tartar.
2. Add butter and use tips of your fingers to mix in with the flour.
3. Add enough ice cold water to make a pastry. Let the pastry rest in the refrigerator for 20 minutes.
4. Roll out the pastry and use a cookie cutter (or a glass if you don't have a cookie cutter) to cut circles.
5. Place a ½ teaspoon of apricot jam in the middle of the circle.
6. Use a brush to rub some milk on the edges. Fold the one half of the circle over to the other side. Press down with a fork and smear with a little bit of milk on the outside.
7. Place in a pre-heated oven of 180°C and bake for about 15 minutes until light brown.

13.12   MERINGUE ("Skuimpies")

Ingredients
4 egg whites
1 ¼ cups castor sugar
½ teaspoon salt
2 teaspoons baking powder
1 teaspoon vanilla extract
Hundreds and thousands

Method
1. Beat the egg whites very well until foamy.
2. Add the castor sugar, a little bit at a time.
3. Fold the salt and baking powder in with the vanilla, and add to the mixture.
4. Press through a piping bag funnel onto a pan, taken out with foil. Sprinkle hundreds and thousands on the top.
5. Bake in the oven on the foil at a low temperature (100°C) for about 20 minutes. Keep an eye so the meringues do not burn (should be crispy).

PS: You can add food colouring to create a variety of coloured meringues. Try out the green, yellow and pink.

13.13 CHOCOLATE TREAT

Ingredients
1 cup butter or margarine
1 egg
2 tablespoons cocoa
3 cups of icing sugar
1 tablespoon vanilla essence
1 packet of Marie biscuits

Method
1. Melt the butter and remove from the heat.
2. Add the beaten egg, cocoa, icing sugar and vanilla.
3. Lastly, crumble the biscuits and add. Mix well.
4. Place in a pan, press down with your fingers and cut into cubes.
5. Leave in the refrigerator and eat when cold.

13.14 " MELKKOS" (Milk food – directly translated)

Ingredients
2 tablespoons hard butter
1 cup flour
Pinch of salt
2 ½ cups milk

Method
1. Rub the butter into the flour using the tips of your fingers.
2. Add the salt and mix.
3. Pour the milk in a saucepan and bring to the boil.
4. Add the flour mixture to the milk a little at a time while stirring with a wooden spoon.
5. Turn the temperature right down and let simmer for about 5 - 10 minutes. Make sure you stir every now and again.
6. Serve the *"melkkos"* in a bowl and sprinkle cinnamon sugar over the top. Mix and enjoy. (Serves about 2)

13.15 "KOEKSISTERS"

Ingredients
½ cup butter/margarine
10 cups cake flour (1 ¼ kg) – start with 8 cups and use more if necessary
6 teaspoons baking powder
1 teaspoon salt
2 cups milk
1 ½ cups water

Method
1. Use finger tips to rub margarine in with the flour, baking powder and salt.
2. Add the rest and knead very well.
3. Cover the dough in a plastic bag and leave at room temperature over night.

Syrup
10 cups sugar   ½ teaspoon ginger
5 cups water   ¼ cup lemon juice

1. Boil the sugar, water and ginger together for 7 minutes.
2. Add the lemon juice the last 2 minutes.
3. Let it cool down and place in the refrigerator until cold on the same day as the dough.

Method
1. The next morning, press the dough down with your fingers and cut into a rectangular form (about the same size as a mustard powder tin). Cut this in half, but don't cut it totally through.
2. Plait the dough and press the ends together.
3. Deep fry in very hot oil until light brown. Take the *"koeksister"* directly from the oil and place it in the syrup so the *"koeksister"* can absorb the syrup. Make sure the syrup stays as cold as possible. When it becomes warm, it won't absorb into the *"koeksister"*.
4. Let it cool down and place in refrigerator. Eat cold!

14. Cookies and Rusks

14.1 BOER'S RUSKS ("Boerbeskuit")

Ingredients (you can use only half the ingredients)

½ cup butter	8 cups flour (then a further 10 cups)
2 ½ cups sugar	1 teaspoon salt
2 ½ cups milk	2 packets of instant yeast
2 eggs	2 cups luke-warm water (with instant yeast)

Method

1. Melt the butter, sugar and milk together. Beat the eggs and add.
2. Mix the yeast with the 2 cups of water (add another ½ cup if necessary).
3. Add the 8 cups of flour (1 at a time), salt and the yeast in with the mixture and knead the dough well.
4. Close and leave as warm as possible (cover with a blanket) for about 3 to 4 hours to rise.
5. Knead the dough and add another 10 cups of flour (1 at a time until the dough is about the same consistency as bread dough).
6. Leave the dough overnight, covered in a blanket to rise (make sure the dough is warmly covered) and bake the next morning.
7. Roll the dough into balls and place in a loaf tin very closely against each other. Let the dough stand in the loaf tin for about an hour.
8. After an hour, place in the oven and bake at 180°C for about an hour.
9. Break the *"beskuit"* (rusks) into pieces and place back in the oven to dry out. The oven must be cool on about 100°C. Leave until golden yellow.
10. The *"beskuit"* can be placed in the oven overnight at a very low temperature, or at a higher temperature for a shorter period. Make sure you keep an eye so it doesn't burn.

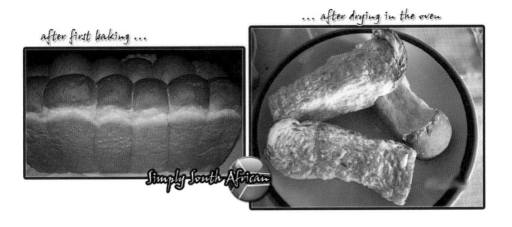

... after drying in the oven

after first baking ...

Simply South African

14.2 BUTTERMILK RUSKS

Rusks taste lovely and stay fresh for a long time. It descends from the French *biscotte*, German *zwieback* and Dutch *rusk*. *"Beskuit"* (rusks) are balls of dough made with yeast, placed in a loaf tin and baked in the oven. It is then removed from the oven and broken up separately. Then it is returned to the oven to dry out for a few hours. The best way to enjoy *"beskuit"* is by dunking it in your tea or coffee for breakfast in the morning.

Ingredients

2 cups margarine	3 teaspoons baking powder
1 ½ cups sugar	½ tablespoon salt
3 eggs	½ tablespoon vinegar
12 cups (1 ½ kg) self-raising flour	2 cups (500ml) buttermilk

Method

1. Mix the butter and sugar very well together and add beaten eggs.
2. Sieve the flour, baking powder and salt together and add.
3. Lastly mix the vinegar with a cup of buttermilk and add this to the mixture. Start with only one cup. Make sure the dough is not runny.
4. Roll into little balls and place them closely against each other in a loaf tin. Let it stand for 30 minutes before baking in a pre-heated oven of 180°C. Bake for 45 minutes to an hour.
5. Remove from the oven and break the rusks apart. Place in a cool oven of about 100°C. Leave overnight or keep an eye on it during the day at a higher heat. Remove from the oven when the rusks are dried.

14.3 OLD FASHIONED SWEET COOKIES

Ingredients

8 cups flour
Pinch of salt
2 teaspoons cream of tartar
2 cups sugar
1 teaspoon fine cloves
2 teaspoons fine cinnamon powder
1 teaspoon ginger

½ cup margarine
2 eggs
2 tablespoons sweet wine
1½ teaspoons bicarbonate of soda
¼ cup water

Method
1. Sieve the flour, salt, and cream of tartar together and add the sugar and spices. Rub the butter into the flour mixture with your fingertips
2. Beat the eggs and wine together and add.
3. Mix the bicarbonate of soda with the water and add.
4. Let the dough rest for about 30 minutes before you use it.
5. Pre-heat the oven to 200°C. Roll little balls with the dough and place on a baking tray. Press lightly down with a fork. You can also use a little cake form to press the dough out with.
6. Bake for about 10 minutes. Make sure the cookies don't burn.

14.4 1-2-3 EASY TO MAKE "SOET" COOKIES (sweet)

Ingredients

5 cups sugar
2 cups margarine (at room temperature)
5 large eggs
9 cups flour
1 cup desiccated coconut
1 tablespoon bicarbonate of soda
1 tablespoon cream of tartar
1 tablespoon baking powder

Method
1. Cream the sugar and soft butter together.
2. Beat the eggs and add.
3. Add 3 cups of flour and coconut to the mixture.
4. Add the rest of the ingredients and mix well.
5. Roll the dough into balls and place on baking tray. Press lightly with a fork.
6. Bake in a pre-heated oven at 180°C on the bottom rack of the oven for about 10 minutes and then the top rack for another 10 minutes.

14.5 COFFEE COOKIES

Ingredients
2 cups butter
2 cups sugar
1 cup of smooth apricot jam
1 tablespoon bicarbonate of soda

1 tablespoon strong instant coffee
Boiling water – to dissolve coffee in
1 ½ teaspoons vanilla extract
8 cups flour

Method
1. Cream the butter and sugar very well and add the apricot jam. Mix well.
2. Then add the bicarbonate of soda that you mixed with a little bit of milk.
3. Dissolve the coffee (Ricoffy or Nescafe) in the water and then add the vanilla.
4. Lastly add the flour and knead very well.
5. Put the dough through the Kenwood mixer or roll out the dough. Cut the dough into rectangular shapes using a pastry wheel.
6. Place onto a baking tray and bake in a pre-heated oven at 180°C. Bake for 10 minutes on the bottom rack and then a further 10 minutes on the top rack.
7. Let them cool down and then use the filling to stick two together.

Filling
1 cup sugar
½ cup butter
1/3 cup milk

1 tablespoon coffee powder
1 teaspoon vanilla extract

1. Boil all the ingredients together for 5 minutes. Remove from heat. Mix with a wooden spoon until the mixture is thick. Let it cool down while stirring.
2. Place in the refrigerator the day before baking.

14.6 RICE CRISPY COOKIES

Ingredients

1 ½ cups margarine
2 cups castor sugar
2 eggs
2 cups desiccated coconut
2 cups oats

2 cups rice Crispies
2 teaspoons baking powder
3 ½ cups flour
½ teaspoon salt
1 teaspoon vanilla extract

Method
1. Cream the butter and sugar together.
2. Add the beaten eggs and mix.
3. Add all the other ingredients and mix well.
4. Roll into little balls and place on baking tray. Press down lightly with a spoon (or you can cut the cookies in blocks with a knife).
5. Bake in a pre-heated oven at 180°C on the bottom rack for about 10 minutes. Then bake it on the top rack for another 10 minutes. Make sure the cookies don't burn.

14.7 OATS COOKIES

Ingredients

1 ½ cups sugar
1 cup butter
2 eggs
1 ½ tablespoons syrup
1 teaspoon bicarbonate of soda (mixed with a little bit of water)
2 ½ cups flour
2 ½ cups desiccated coconut
2 ½ cups oats
Pinch of salt

Method
1. Cream the sugar and butter very well together.
2. Add the beaten eggs and syrup to the mixture. Add the bicarbonate of soda.
3. Add the rest of the ingredients and mix well.
4. Roll into little balls and place on a baking tray. Lightly press down with a fork.
5. Bake in a pre-heated oven at 190°C for 10 to 20 minutes.
6. Start by baking it on the bottom rack and then moving it up to the top rack (about 10 minutes on each).

14.8 GINGER COOKIES

Ingredients
½ cup margarine
1 ¼ cups brown sugar
1 egg
½ cup golden syrup
2 ½ cups flour
1 tablespoon bicarbonate of soda
1 tablespoon cream of tartar
3 teaspoons ginger
Pinch of salt

Method
1. Cream the margarine and sugar together.
2. Add the egg and syrup.
3. Mix the rest of the ingredients with the butter mix.
4. Roll the dough into little balls, place on a baking tray and press down lightly with a spoon.
5. Bake in a pre-heated oven at 200°C. First bake on the bottom rack for about 10 minutes and then the top rack for another 10 minutes. Make sure it doesn't burn.

14.9 PEANUT BUTTER COOKIES

Ingredients
½ cup butter
¼ cup white sugar
½ cup brown sugar
½ cup peanut butter (smooth peanut butter is better to use)
1 egg
1 ¼ cups flour
Pinch of salt
½ teaspoon bicarbonate of soda, dissolved in a ¼ cup of milk

Method
1. Mix the butter, sugar and peanut butter.
2. Then add the egg.
3. Sieve the flour and salt together and add.
4. Lastly add the bicarbonate of soda.
5. Roll into little balls and place on a baking plate. Press down lightly with a spoon.
6. Bake for about 15 minutes in a cool oven at 150°C.

14.10 APRICOT COOKIES

Ingredients
1 cup butter
1 ½ cups sugar
1 teaspoon bicarbonate of soda mixed with a little bit of water
1 cup apricot jam
2 eggs
4 cups flour
1 teaspoon ginger
1 teaspoon cinnamon

Method
1. Cream the butter and sugar together.
2. Add the bicarbonate of soda and jam.
3. Beat the eggs, add and mix.
4. Add the rest of the ingredients and mix. Let the dough rest for about 15 minutes before baking.
5. Roll the dough into little balls and place on a baking tray.
6. Lightly press down with a fork.
7. Place on the bottom rack in a pre-heated oven at 180°C for about 10 minutes.
8. Move the pan up to the top rack and bake for about another 10 minutes until lightly brown.
9. Remove and let it cool down.
10. Stick 2 cookies together by using apricot jam.

14.11 CUSTARD COOKIES

Ingredients
2 cups butter/margarine
2 cups sugar
3 eggs
1 cup custard powder
2 cups cornflour
4 cups flour
3 teaspoons baking powder
½ teaspoon salt
1 teaspoon vanilla extract

Method
1. Cream the butter and sugar together.
2. Add the eggs, custard powder, cornflour, flour, baking powder and salt.
3. Lastly add the vanilla and mix well.
4. Roll out the dough and cut into rectangular shapes. Should be about the same size as a mustard tin.
5. Bake in a pre-heated oven at 190°C. Make sure you bake on the bottom rack of the oven first and then the top rack. Total baking time is about 10 minutes on each rack. Make sure the cookies don't burn.

Filling
1 cup sugar
½ cup butter/margarine
½ cup milk
1 tablespoon custard
1 teaspoon vanilla extract

1. Boil all the ingredients together for 5 minutes. After you have removed the mixture from the stove, mix it with a wooden spoon until the mixture becomes thicker. Let it cool down.
2. Place in the refrigerator the day before you bake the cookies.

14.12 APRICOT SQUARES

Ingredients
½ cup butter
½ cup sugar
1 egg
Pinch of salt
2 cups flour
2 teaspoons baking powder

Method
1. Cream together the butter and sugar
2. Add the egg and mix well. Then sieve the salt, flour and baking powder together and add. Mix well together and divide the dough.
3. Press ¾ of the dough in a baking plate and put the rest in the refrigerator.
4. Spread apricot jam over the dough and grate the other ¼ of the dough over the top.
5. Bake in a pre-heated oven at 180ºC for 25 minutes.
6. Cut into squares and enjoy!

14.13 CHERRY AND RICE CRISPY COOKIES

Ingredients
1 cup butter
1 cup castor sugar
1 egg
1 teaspoon vanilla extract
2 ½ cups self raising flour
A pinch of salt
2 cups desiccated coconut
Cherries
Rice Crispies

Method
1. Cream the butter and sugar together.
2. Add the egg and vanilla and mix well.
3. Sieve the flour and salt together. Then add the coconut.
4. Mix well and roll into little balls.
5. Roll these balls in the crushed Rice Crispies.
6. Place on a baking plate, press down with a spoon and place a ¼ of a cherry on top.
7. Bake in a pre-heated oven at 180ºC for about 10 minutes.

14.14 "SOENTJIES" (Kisses)

Ingredients

2 cups margarine
2 cups sugar
3 eggs
4 cups flour

3 cups cornflour
3 teaspoons baking powder
½ teaspoon salt

Method

1. Cream the butter and sugar together and add the beaten eggs.
2. Sieve the dry ingredients together and add in turn with the eggs.
3. Knead well and put through the Kenwood mixer. If you don't have a mixer, press the dough and cut into rectangular shapes with a pastry cutter.
4. Bake on the bottom rack in a pre-heated oven at 180°C for 10 minutes and then a further 10 minutes on the top rack. Be careful, they do easily burn.

Filling

1 cup sugar
½ cup butter

½ cup milk
1 teaspoon vanilla extract

1. Boil all the ingredients together for about 5 minutes.
2. After you have removed the mixture from the stove, mix it with a wooden spoon until the mixture becomes thicker. Let it cool down.
3. Place in the refrigerator the day before you bake the cookies.

14.15 JAN SMUTS COOKIES

What is very interesting is that the generals used to name cookies after themselves. Why? Because they would have a favourite. This favourite would then be named after a specific general and everybody would know whose favourite the cookies were.

Ingredients for pastry

This is a sugar-based pastry used for the little cups you put the filling in. You can buy pre-made pastry or make your own. This is a basic recipe

½ cup butter
2 ½ cups flour
Pinch of salt
½ cup sugar
2 teaspoons baking powder
1 beaten egg

Method

1. Rub the butter into the flour and salt with your fingertips.
2. Add the sugar, baking powder and egg.
3. Roll out the dough and use a cookie cutter to press it out with. Place in little muffin pans (you can also use bigger pans).
4. Place a little spoon full of apricot jam/preserves in the empty shell (pastry).

Filling

½ cup sugar
½ cup margarine
2 well-beaten eggs
1 teaspoon baking powder
½ - ¾ cup flour (use ½ cup at first, only use more if it is too runny)

1. Cream the sugar and margarine (at room temperature) together. Add the rest of the ingredients and mix until creamy.
2. Place one teaspoon of this filling on top of the apricot jam and bake it in a pre-heated oven at 180°C for about 15 minutes until light brown.
3. Remove the cookies and place on a cooling rack.

14.16 HOME-MADE ROMANY CREAMS

Ingredients
1 ½ cups butter/margarine
1 ½ cups sugar
3 cups flour
2 ¼ cups desiccated coconut
2 teaspoons baking powder
Pinch of salt
4 tablespoons cocoa powder
¼ cup boiling water
1 slab of dark chocolate (you can also use milk chocolate)

Method
1. Cream the butter and sugar together.
2. Add the flour, coconut, baking powder and salt. Mix well.
3. Dissolve the cocoa in the boiling water.
4. Add this to the dough.
5. Mix well. Let the dough stand for about 15 minutes before use.
6. Use your hands to roll little balls.
7. Place in a buttered pan and press lightly down with a fork.
8. Bake for 10 minutes in a pre-heated oven at 180°C on the bottom rack of the oven. Move the pan to the top rack for a further 10 minutes. Make sure it doesn't burn.
9. Melt the chocolate over water on the stove and use this to stick 2 cookies together.

14.17 GENERAL HERTZOG COOKIES

Ingredients for pastry
2 cups flour
Pinch of salt
2 teaspoons baking powder
½ cup margarine
3 eggs (white and yellow separate)
1 ½ tablespoons sugar
If the pastry is too thick, add about 2 tablespoons of milk.

Method
1. Sieve the flour, salt and baking powder together.
2. Rub the margarine into the flour mixture with your fingertips.
3. Add the egg yolks and the sugar. Mix. Let it stand for about 15 minutes.
4. Roll out the dough and place in a little muffin pan (can also be a bigger pan).
5. Place a small teaspoon of apricot jam in the pastry.

Filling
1. Beat the egg whites very well.
2. Add ½ cup sugar and 1 cup of desiccated coconut to the egg whites and place a spoon full on top of the apricot jam.
3. Bake in a pre-heated oven at 180°C until light brown on top, for about 10 to 20 minutes.

15. Bread

15.1 DATE BREAD ("Dadelbrood")

Ingredients
1 packet (250g) of dates (remove pits and cut in half)
2 cups boiling water
2 teaspoons bicarbonate of soda
2 cups sugar
½ cup butter/margarine
3 eggs
1 teaspoon vanilla extract
4 cups flour
1 teaspoon salt
1 teaspoon baking powder

Method
1. Place the dates in a bowl with the boiling water and bicarbonate of soda. Let it cool down.
2. Cream the sugar and butter together. Then add the eggs and vanilla and mix.
3. Sieve the flour, salt and baking powder together and add.
4. Lastly add to the date mixture and mix well.
5. Place in a loaf tin and bake in a pre-heated oven at 180°C for 1 hour.

15.2 RAISIN BREAD

Ingredients
4 cups flour
3 teaspoons baking powder
1 teaspoon salt
1 ½ tablespoons sugar
½ cup raisins
1 cup milk
1 ½ tablespoons butter

Method
1. Sieve the flour, baking powder and salt together.
2. Add the sugar, raisins, milk and melted butter.
3. Mix well and place in a bread pan.
4. Bake in a pre-heated oven at 180°C for 1 hour.

15.3 BANANA BREAD

Ingredients
½ cup butter
1 cup sugar
1 teaspoon vanilla extract
2 eggs
2 cups flour
2 teaspoons baking powder
Pinch of salt
5 small bananas (or 3 large bananas)

Method
1. Cream the butter and sugar together and add the vanilla.
2. Mix the eggs in with this, one at a time.
3. Sieve the dry ingredients together and add.
4. Lastly mash the bananas and add.
5. Bake for 1 hour in a pre-heated oven at 180°C.

15.4 GINGERBREAD

Ingredients
½ cup butter/margarine
½ cup sugar
1 egg
1 cup syrup
2 ½ cups flour
1 teaspoon ginger
1 teaspoon mixed spices
1 teaspoon of fine cloves
1 cup warm water
1 ½ teaspoons bicarbonate of soda

Method
1. Cream the butter and sugar together.
2. Beat the egg and add. Mix well.
3. Add the syrup.
4. Sieve together the flour, ginger, mixed spices and fine cloves. Add.
5. Then add the water and mix.
6. Lastly add the bicarbonate of soda mixed with a little bit of milk.
7. Bake in a loaf tin in a pre-heated oven at 180°C for 35 minutes
8. Serve the gingerbread with butter.

15.5 MEALY BREAD

Ingredients
3 eggs
½ cup sugar
1 cup flour
3 teaspoons baking powder
Pinch of salt
1 cup maize meal
1 small tin of sweet corn

Method
1. Beat the eggs. Then add the rest of the ingredients and mix well.
2. Pour in a loaf tin. Place the pan in a big saucepan with boiling water.
3. Let it steam in the closed pan for about 20 minutes. If the water vaporises, more can be added after 10 minutes.

16. Preserves

Fig Jam

Simply South African

In the earlier years, people did not know that some bacteria could kill them, so when they came up with new ideas to preserve food, it was only to make sure the food lasted for as long as possible. What happened is they discovered 2 ways in which they could preserve foods. The first way was to boil food with certain spices or ingredients that would keep it from going off and the other way was to dry it in the sun.

South Africa is as famous for its dried fruit as it is for its dried meat. "Biltong" is a great example of dried meat enjoyed by everyone while jam is a good example of preserved fruit.

The idea of jam was probably brought over by the French. The *"Voortrekkers"* used this idea by adding a syrup after steaming the fruits as well as some spices, then placing it in glass jars to last. Fig preserve is the most famous and is delicious with cheese!

16.1 APRICOT PRESERVE

Ingredients
Apricots
Sugar (*500g of sugar should be used for every 500g of apricots*)
Water (*Add 1 cup of water for every 500g of apricots*)
Salt

Method
1. Open the apricots and remove the pits. Apricots must be ripe, but a few can be a little less ripe. That will help the preserve to go a bit thicker.
2. Place apricots in salty water (2 teaspoons of salt in 5 litres of water) overnight.
3. The next morning the apricots need to be dried very well. They can be dried by placing it in the sun for a little while.
4. Weigh the apricots to determine how much sugar you will have to use.
5. Place the sugar and fruit in a big saucepan. Add 1 cup of water for every 500g of fruit. Stir continuously.
6. Make sure the sugar is dissolved before you bring the mixture to the boil. Add a few pits from the apricots for flavour.
7. Boil for about 1 ½ hours while leaving the lid off and stir every now and again.
8. Place the preserve into glass jars while warm. Leave for a while and then add the lid.

16.2 WATERMELON PRESERVE

Ingredients
Watermelon skin
Water *(3 cups of water for every 500g of watermelon skin)*
Bicarbonate of soda
Sugar *(use 500g of sugar for every 500g of watermelon skin)*
Ginger
Lemon juice
Salt

Method
1. Peel the green outside of the watermelon skin, firstly prick the skins with a fork and cut into blocks. Weigh the skins and place them in water mixed with 3 teaspoons of bicarbonate of soda. Leave it covered in water over night.
2. Wash the skin the next morning very well (rinse about 4 times).
3. Make a syrup using 500g of sugar for every 500g of watermelon skin. 3 cups of water need to be added for every 500g of watermelon skin. (Make sure that the water is enough to cover the skins).
4. Boil the sugar and water together and add 2 teaspoons of ginger. Add 1 tablespoon of lemon juice and a pinch of salt.
5. Add the fruit and stir. Boil for about 1 to 2 hours until the skin becomes see-through.
6. Place the preserve in glass jars when it has cooled down.

16.3 GUAVA PRESERVE

Ingredients

500g guavas

Water

½ cup lemon juice

375g sugar

Method

1. Peal the skin of the guavas and cut in half. Scoop the pits out with a teaspoon and keep separately in a pot. Cut the fruit into smaller pieces.
2. Boil the fruit in a little bit of water until soft. Boil the pits separate in a little bit of water. Put this through a fine sieve and add to the fruit.
3. Boil the fruit together with the lemon juice and sugar (375g of sugar for every 500g of guavas). Boil until sugar has dissolved and the mixture is thicker.
4. Place in bottles while warm. After it has cooled down, cover with paper that has been dunked in a little bit of brandy (optional).

16.4 PEACH CHUTNEY

Ingredients

1kg yellow peaches (take out the pits and dice)

2 cups vinegar

2 onions (chopped finely)

1 cup raisins (optional)

1 cup sugar

1 tablespoon red pepper

½ teaspoon salt

2 teaspoons coriander

1 teaspoon mustard

½ teaspoon turmeric

Method

1. Place all of the ingredients in a pan and warm up until sugar has dissolved.
2. Simmer until the chutney becomes thicker and the peaches are soft.
3. Place warm in bottles and put away.

16.5 MARMALADE

Ingredients (amount of fruit depends on how much marmalade you want)

1 orange

1 lemon

1 grapefruit

Water

Sugar

Method

1. Mince all the fruits together (use as much fruit as you like).
2. Use 3 cups of water for every cup of fruit. Boil until soft.
3. Use 1 cup of sugar for every cup of fruit and water mix.
4. Boil until a jelly is formed.
5. Place in glass bottles while warm and cover with lid.

16.6 GREEN FIG PRESERVE

Ingredients
Figs
Water *(use 2 cups of water for every cup of sugar)*
Bicarbonate of soda
Sugar *(use 500g of sugar for every 500g of figs)*
Cloves
Cinnamon
Ginger
Lemon juice

Method
1. Peel the skin of the figs and make a little cross cut on the flower end.
2. Place the fruit in water, mixed with 2 tablespoons of bicarbonate of soda for every 16 cups of water. Let it soak in water overnight.
3. Rinse the figs the next morning with water and place in boiling water for 15 minutes until soft. Drain off the water.
4. Place the figs in a syrup made up with 500g of sugar for every 500g of figs. Use 2 cups of water for every cup of sugar.
5. Add a few whole cloves, 1 teaspoon of cinnamon, 1 teaspoon of ginger and 4 tablespoons of lemon juice for every 3kg of fruit.
6. Boil quickly for 2 hours until the syrup goes thick. Place figs in glass jars with tight lids.

17. Tarts

17.1 CREMORA TART

South Africans celebrate birthdays by baking!! Chocolate cake, banana bread and TARTS. This is the highlight of the year, having a day with absolutely great baking, eating anything you like.

Ingredients
2 ½ cups cremora (coffee creamer)
1 cup ice cold water
1 tin (397g) condensed milk
¾ cup lemon juice
1 pack tennis biscuits (or any coconut biscuits)

Method
1. Mix the cremora very well with the water.
2. Add the condensed milk to the mixture and beat well.
3. Add the lemon juice and mix very well.
4. Place the biscuits at the bottom as a base. Pour the above mixture in the pan and crumble some biscuits over the top.

PS: to give extra taste, you can add a small tin of crushed pineapples.

17.2 GUAVA FRIDGE TART

Ingredients
1 large tin of guavas
1 ½ tablespoons sugar
3 tablespoons custard powder
¼ cup lemon juice
1 tin condensed milk
1 apricot Swiss roll
1 tin of cream

Method
1. Cut the guavas into pieces and mix it with the sugar.
2. Mix the custard powder with a little bit of the guava syrup.
3. Boil the mixture until thick while continuously stirring, and let it cool down.
4. Beat the lemon juice and the condensed milk until thick.
5. Cut the Swiss roll into slices and place in the bottom of the bowl.
6. Pour the guava mix on top of the Swiss roll.
7. Lastly beat the cream and pour on top just before serving.

17.3 MILK TART ("Melktert")

Ingredients (sugar pastry for milk tart)
½ cup butter/margarine

½ cup sugar

1 egg

2 cups flour

2 teaspoons baking powder

Salt

Method
1. Cream the butter and sugar together, then add the egg.
2. Sieve the dry ingredients together and add. Mix together.
3. Place in two pans (enough to make 4) and bake at 160°C until light brown (about 10 to 20 minutes). – ½ the quantity is enough to make 2 tarts.

Ingredients for filling
3 tablespoons butter

4 ½ cups milk

3 tablespoons flour

3 tablespoons cornflour

½ cup sugar

Salt

3 eggs

Method
1. Boil the butter and milk together.
2. Mix the flour, cornflour, sugar and salt.
3. Beat the eggs and add to the flour mixture. Mix until it is smooth.
4. Pour half of the milk mixture in with the flour mixture and mix. Then add it back with the rest of the milk and let it boil until the mixture becomes thicker. Boil at a low heat. Mix with a spoon so it doesn't burn.
5. Divide the mixture between the two pastries you prepared.
6. Sprinkle cinnamon on top.

17.4 PINEAPPLE TART

Ingredients for pastry (makes 2)
1½ tablespoons butter
1 tablespoon sugar
1 egg
1 teaspoon baking powder
3 tablespoons flour
Pinch of salt

Method
1. Cream the butter and sugar together.
2. Add the beaten egg and mix. Add the rest of the ingredients.
3. Place in the pans and bake in a pre-heated oven at 180°C for about 10 minutes until light brown.

Ingredients for filling
1 tin of pineapple pieces
½ cup water
1 packet of lemon jelly powder

1 tin of condensed milk
1 cup of cream
1 teaspoon vanilla extract

Method
1. Pour the syrup of the pineapple in a pan with ½ cup of water and boil together.
2. Add this to the packet of jelly and make sure the jelly dissolves.
3. Add the condensed milk and mix well.
4. Add the pineapple and let it cool down. Pour into the pastry.
5. Beat the cream together with the vanilla and smear on top of the tart. Place in the refrigerator to cool down.

17.5 PEPPERMINT CRISP TART

Ingredients
1 cup of Orley Whip (or cream if you don't have Orley Whip)
1 tin (397g) carnation treat (or boiled condensed milk)
1 slab Peppermint Crisp (or peppermint chocolate)
1 packet of tennis biscuits (or coconut biscuits)

Method
1. Beat the cream until thick. Add the boiled condensed milk (boil for about 3 hours) and ½ of the grated peppermint crisp.
2. Pack one layer of biscuits, a layer of mixture, one layer of biscuits and another layer of mixture. Grate the rest of the Peppermint Crisp on top of the tart.

17.6 APPLE TART

Ingredients
3 tablespoons butter
1 cup sugar
1 teaspoon vanilla extract
2 eggs
1 cup flour

1 teaspoon baking powder
Pinch of salt
¼ cup milk
1 tin of tart apples

Method
1. Cream the butter and sugar together.
2. Add the vanilla and beaten eggs. Mix well.
3. Sieve the flour, baking powder and salt
4. Mix all the ingredients together with a ¼ cup of milk.
5. Place the mixture in two round pans.
6. Place the tart apples in the tart mixture and place both pans in a pre-heated oven at 200°C for 30 minutes.

Syrup
1 cup sugar
½ cup butter
¾ cup milk

1. Mix all the ingredients together and boil for 5 minutes.
2. Pour this syrup warm over the 2 tarts when you remove it from the oven. The syrup has to be absorbed into the tarts.
3. Can be served as it is or with cream.

17.7 YOGHURT TART

Ingredients
1 pack of tennis biscuits (coconut biscuits)
Little bit of butter.
4 cups of plain yoghurt
1 tin (397g) condensed milk
1 cup of cream
1 pack vanilla instant pudding

Method
1. Crush the biscuits fine and mix with the melted butter.
2. Use as a base for the tart.
3. Beat the rest of the ingredients together.
4. Pour in the crust and place in the refrigerator. Serve cold.

17.8 MARSHMALLOW TART

Ingredients
1 tin (397g) condensed milk
½ cup lemon juice
12 red cherries cut in half
1 pack (125g) of marshmallows (finely cut)
1 cup cream
1 teaspoon of vanilla extract
Small tin of crushed pineapples
1 pack of tennis biscuits (or any coconut biscuit)

Method
1. Mix the condensed milk and lemon juice and leave it for a few minutes to get a bit thicker.
2. Add the cherries and the marshmallows.
3. Beat the cream and vanilla extract until stiff and add.
4. Pineapples are added lastly (don't use the syrup). Mix very well.
5. Pack a layer of biscuits and add the mixture on top.
6. Crumble some biscuits on top of the tart.

17.9 TIPSY TART

Ingredients (makes 2 tarts)
¾ cup boiling water
1 teaspoon bicarbonate of soda
¾ cup dates (cut up)
½ cup butter
¾ cup sugar
2 eggs
1 ½ cups flour
½ teaspoon baking powder
¾ cup crushed nuts

Method
1. Add the boiling water and bicarbonate of soda to ½ the dates. Let it cool down.
2. Cream the butter and sugar. Add the beaten eggs and mix well.
3. Sieve the flour and baking powder together and add to the mixture.
4. Then add the rest of the dates and the nuts.
5. Add the dates in water last. Mix well. Pour into two round tart pans.
6. Bake in a pre-heated oven at 200°C for 20 – 30 minutes.

Syrup
1 ¼ cups sugar
1 tablespoon butter
¾ cup water
2 teaspoons vanilla extract
½ cup brandy

1. Boil the sugar, butter and water together for 5 minutes.
2. Then add the vanilla and ½ cup of brandy.
3. Boil for another 2 minutes.
4. Pour the sauce over the tarts once it comes out of the oven, while hot.
5. Serve with cream on top

17.10 SAVOURY TART ("Souttert")

Ingredients
2 eggs
1 cup milk
2 cups of grated cheese
3 viennas (or hot dog sausages, cut into pieces)
1 tablespoon grated onion
1 teaspoon parsley
1 teaspoon mustard powder
Pinch of salt
¼ cup flour

Method
1. Beat the eggs and add the rest of the ingredients.
2. Mix well and pour into a round tart pan.
3. Bake in a pre-heated oven at 160°C for one hour.
4. Serve warm.

18. Cakes

Fruit Cake

Simply South African

18.1 CHOCOLATE CAKE

Chocolate cake is best enjoyed when carnation treat (boiled condensed milk) is used as icing. Boil the condensed milk for about 3 hours, smear on the cooled down cake and sprinkle a broken snowflake on the top. Tastes lovely.

Ingredients
½ cup butter
¾ cup boiling milk
½ cup of cocoa
2 teaspoons vanilla extract
¼ cup boiling water
4 extra large eggs (whites and yolks separate)
1 ¼ cups sugar
1 ¾ cups flour
3 teaspoons baking powder
Pinch of salt

Method
1. Melt the butter in boiling milk.
2. Add the cocoa and vanilla to the boiling water.
3. Add the milk and water mixture together. Mix well and let it cool down.
4. Beat the egg whites until stiff. Add the yolks of the eggs and mix.
5. Add the sugar and beat well.
6. Sieve the flour, baking powder and salt together and add to the egg mixture. Make sure you mix very well.
7. Take the cooled down milk and cocoa mixture from the start and add to the rest. Fold into the mixture with a wooden spoon.
8. Pour this mixture into an oven pan and bake in a pre-heated oven at 180°C for about 35 minutes.

18.2 FRUIT CAKE (Microwave)

Ingredients

A: 1 pack (500g) of fruit cake mix   ½ cup margarine
       1 pack (250g) of dates   1 cup warm tap water
       1 cup brown sugar   2 teaspoons chocolate colouring

B: 2 teaspoons of bicarbonate of soda   1 teaspoon of mixed spices
       1 packet (250g) of cherries   Pinch of salt
       2 cups self-raising flour   3 eggs
       1 cup of nuts   1 cup of brandy

Method

1. Mix the ingredients from A well and cook in the microwave for 5 minutes.
2. Mix very well and cook for a further 4 minutes.
3. Add 2 teaspoons bicarbonate of soda and leave to cool down.
4. Add the cherries, flour, nuts, mixed spices, salt, eggs and ½ cup of brandy.
5. Add to the above mixture and mix very well.
6. Place in a ring pan and bake for 14 minutes in the microwave on high. Let it cool down for 4 minutes and pour another ½ cup of brandy over the cake.
7. Let it cool down and wrap in foil. Mixture is enough to make 2 ring cakes.

18.3 SPONGE CAKE

This mixture can be used to bake one big cake and you can use regular icing sugar mixed with margarine and then sprinkle with hundreds and thousands. The same mixture can also be used to bake little individual cup cakes.

Ingredients
1 cup margarine
1 ½ cups sugar
1 cup cornflour
1 cup milk
4 eggs
2 cups flour
2 teaspoons baking powder
Pinch of salt
1 teaspoon vanilla extract
1 teaspoon grated orange skin

Method
1. Cream the butter and sugar together.
2. Mix the cornflour with ½ cup of milk and add.
3. Beat the eggs very well and add to the mixture.
4. Sieve the flour, baking powder and salt together and add this in turn with the rest of the milk.
5. Add the vanilla and orange skin lastly. Mix well and pour into a round pan.
6. Bake in a pre-heated oven at 180°C for about 50 minutes (until light brown).

18.4 CARROT CAKE

Ingredients
1 cup sugar
1 cup sunflower oil
3 eggs
1 ½ cups flour
2 teaspoons baking powder
Pinch of salt

½ teaspoon bicarbonate of soda
2 teaspoons cinnamon
3 small bananas
1 cup grated carrots
½ cup walnuts

Method
1. Cream together the sugar, oil and eggs.
2. Sieve the flour, baking powder, salt, bicarbonate of soda and cinnamon together.
3. Add the mashed bananas, carrots and walnuts.
4. Mix very well and bake for 30 – 40 minutes in a pre-heated oven at 180°C.

Icing for the carrot cake
½ cup creamed cheese
½ cup butter

4 cups of icing sugar
1 teaspoon vanilla extract

1. Mix all the ingredients together and smear on top of the carrot cake, after it has cooled down.
2. Take some walnuts and sprinkle it on top.

THANKS AGAIN…

Thank you very much for sharing this recipe book… It is fantastic to know that other people have the same opportunity to enjoy the recipes as much as my husband and myself!

Don't forget to visit my site at:

www.RecipesFromSouthAfrica.com/Videos

to check out our videos.

Cook, bake, eat and enjoy AND remember to always share these great times.

5033768R10077

Printed in Great Britain
by Amazon.co.uk, Ltd.,
Marston Gate.